WOMEN CALLED TO WITNESS

WOMEN
C A L L E D   T O
WITNESS

Evangelical Feminism in the 19th Century

NANCY A. HARDESTY

ABINGDON PRESS

Nashville

WOMEN CALLED TO WITNESS

Copyright © 1984 by Abingdon Press

Library of Congress Cataloging in Publication Data

HARDESTY, NANCY.
  Women called to witness.
  Bibliography: p.
  Includes index.
  1. Evangelicalism—United States—History—19th century. 2. Women
in Christianity—United States—History—19th century. 3. Revivals—
United States—History—19th century. 4. United States—Church his-
tory—19th century. I. Title.

BF1642.U5H37 1984   280'.4   83-22395
ISBN 0-687-45959-1

Cover photo of Phoebe Palmer, engraving by H. B. Hall & Sons, 1876, from
The Life and Letters of Mrs. Phoebe Palmer by Rev. Richard Wheatley. New
York: W. C. Palmer, Jr., publisher, 1876. All other photos from *American
Women*, rev. ed., edited by Frances E. Willard and Mary A. Livermore. 2 vols.
New York: Mast, Crowell & Kirkpatrick, 1897.

MANUFACTURED BY THE PARTHENON PRESS AT
NASHVILLE, TENNESSEE, UNITED STATES OF AMERICA

DEDICATED TO

Phoebe
Fletcher
Benjamin
and
Skip

$\mathcal{W}$e hear enough about our forefathers. They were nice old fellows, no doubt. Perfect bricks in their way. Good to work, eat or fight. But where are their companions? Our foremothers. Who landed at James River and came over on the *Mayflower* and established the other early settlements? Were there any women among men? One would think not. . . . All hail to noble old boys, our forefathers say we. May the glory of their deeds never be less, but the good book tells us to "render unto Caesar," etc., and we wish to speak a word in season for women generally and especially for our noble . . . foremothers lest time and the one-sided page of history shall blot them forever from our memories.

—*Advocate and Family Guardian*
1860

CONTENTS

PREFACE

*N*ineteenth-century American feminism was deeply rooted in evangelical revivalism. Its theology and practice motivated and equipped women and men to adopt a feminist ideology, to reject stereotyped sex roles, and to work for positive changes in marriage, church, society, and politics. Most woman's rights leaders—whether in the church, education, reform organizations, or the media—were products of evangelical backgrounds or were deeply influenced by evangelical culture, whether or not they acknowledged that debt or maintained any allegiance to it in later life.

Feminism can be defined as a belief in and commitment to the moral and social autonomy of individuals male and female. It is a commitment to woman's freedom to choose her own destiny apart from sex-determined roles, society's rules, or any of the social relationships in which she participates. From this belief in "free moral agency" grew the woman's rights movement, with its demands for such rights as control over one's own finances, child custody, divorce, birth control, education, employment opportunity, and ultimately suffrage.

Evangelical is also a word that demands definition and contextualizing. Derived from the Greek word translated "gospel," *euangelion*—"good news"—*evangelical* is related to the Reformation's emphasis on justification by faith. In nineteenth-century America it refers primarily to the cultural milieu created by those groups of people converted in the Second Great Awakening and those who made Methodism the fastest-growing and largest Protestant denomination of the era.

This book is particularly interested in the "Finneyites," those caught up in the revivalism of the 1820s and 1830s which Charles Grandison Finney spread from upstate New York east to New England and west to Ohio. As Keith Melder noted in *Beginnings of Sisterhood:*

> Their sisterhood in faith helped these women to achieve an attitude of self-confidence and a sense of mission that infected many of their later activities. Surely it is no coincidence that the areas where Finney's revivals and women's religious education flourished—New England, upstate New York and northern Ohio—were early centers of women's reform work and feminism.

The revivalists' emphasis on conversion and commitment gave women and men a mission to save the world which applied not only to souls but also to bodies, minds, social relations, and the body politic. The same strategies used in evangelism—the spreading of the gospel per se—were also used to spread the gospel of reform. Just as women learned in Finney's meetings to pray for their unregenerate neighbors by name, so they were not afraid to kneel in front of New York City brothels or Hillsboro, Ohio, saloons and pray for their sinful neighbors by name.

"Turning through time workwoven, the history of women is a world to be fought for," says the poster above my desk. This book seeks to shed some light on the interplay of women's involvement in religion and reform. It tells again the story. Rather than relying on psychological, economic, or sociological insights, it seeks to interpret the words and actions of its actors on their own terms and from within the religious ethos that nurtured them. Certainly Christianity was used by some religious leaders to limit and oppose women's participation in society. Traditionalist conservatives such as Old School Presbyterians, Lutherans, and Episcopalians then, as in our own day, argued against women's ministry and mission. Liberal religion in some areas (as Ann Douglas in *The Feminization of American Culture* and Nancy F. Cott in *The Bonds of Womanhood* have argued) did sentimentalize and trivialize women's contributions, confining them to domesticity. Finneyite revivalism, however, which flowed into the holiness, higher life, and evangelical Unitarian movements of the post–Civil War period, as Timothy Smith noted in *Revivalism and Social Reform,* was the energizing stream, the creative élan of the faith. From it feminists drew their nourishment.

Other women's historians have drawn distinctions between public and domestic, hard and soft, reform and radical feminists. This work does not because such distinctions blur the uniqueness of each woman's contribution to the cause. The women worked in various ways. Some were talkers; some doers; some joiners; some loners—often depending on the demands and commitments of their personal lives at the moment. Thus, for example, the Grimké sisters, Sarah and Angelina, were vocal and very public advocates of abolition and woman's rights in the late 1830s but retired to the domestic circle for the remainder of their long lives, emerging only rarely in speech or print. Feminists also used a variety of rhetorical approaches, determined more by what their audiences might find convincing than by any particular ideological framework. For all her use of the rhetoric of home and motherhood, for example, Frances Willard was no less a strong and effective feminist than Elizabeth Cady Stanton or Susan B. Anthony— nor less radical at times!

Nor is this work confined to the traditional historical periods. Based on American political historians' periodization, many women's historians have concentrated either on antebellum reform or on the post–Civil War drive for suffrage. Initially this work, based on a University of Chicago Divinity School dissertation entitled " 'Your Daughters Shall Prophesy': Revivalism and Feminism in the Age of Finney," was circumscribed by the life of Charles Grandison Finney (1792–1875) and thus centered in antebellum efforts. However, subsequent research made it clear that the spinal cord of the movement ran from women's earliest organizations to promote missions and charity in the early 1800s straight and strong to the passage of the Nineteenth Amendment in 1920. This book traces that lifeline.

I am indebted to my friends Donald W. Dayton and Lucille Sider Dayton for their initial encouragement to pursue this

topic during my graduate studies. Martin E. Marty ably
directed my dissertation, and I am grateful for his counsel and
continued support, along with that of readers Gerald Brauer
and Arthur Mann.

For encouragement through the publication of pieces of
research along the way, I wish to thank Rosemary Radford
Ruether and Eleanor McLoughlin, editors of *Women of Spirit:
Female Leadership in the Jewish and Christian Traditions;* my
Emory University Candler School of Theology colleague
Theodore Runyon, editor of *Sanctification and Liberation:
Liberation Theologies in Light of the Wesleyan Tradition;* and
Hilah F. Thomas and Rosemary Skinner Keller, editors of
*Women in New Worlds: Historical Perspectives on the Wesleyan
Tradition.*

My mother, Ruth Parr Hardesty, deserves special thanks for
her continual prodding and for her own research into our family
history, which stretches back across Ohio, Pennsylvania,
Virginia, and New Jersey to the Revolutionary War. It was she
who unearthed two bits of paper which give me a special feeling
of connectedness with those of whom I write: a receipt for a
contribution to the Prohibition Party bearing the slogan, No
citizen shall be denied the right to vote on account of sex,
and a receipt from *The Lima Clipper,* "The only paper in
Northwestern Ohio that advocates Equal Suffrage, Prohibition
of the Liquor Traffic and a single standard of morals for men
and women." Both bear the name of Joseph Tapscott, my
paternal great-grandfather.

A final word of gratitude to those special friends who have
stood by me and encouraged me along the way: Letha Dawson
Scanzoni, Evelyn Monahan, Robinette Kennedy, and Patricia
Strickland.

CHAPTER 1

WOMAN OF THE CENTURY

*. . . honestly, I always thought that, next to a wish I
had to be a saint some day, I really would like to be a
politician.*

—*Frances E. Willard*

*D*inner finished, the family gathered in front of the
fire. "I heard in Janesville today that Maine has passed a law
prohibiting the sale of liquor," announced Josiah Willard. "I
wonder if poor, rum-cursed Wisconsin will ever get a law like
that?"

"Yes, Josiah, there'll be such a law all over the land some
day, when women vote," Mary, his wife, replied.

"And pray how will you arrange it so that women shall vote?"
he queried sarcastically, astonished to hear such talk from his
wife.

Her eyes focused on the fire, and the rocker moved more
quickly: "Well, I say to you, as the apostle Paul said to his jailor,
'You have put us into prison, we being Romans, and you must
come and take us out.' "

Though only eleven years old on that night in 1851, Frances
Willard long remembered her parents' conversation. She also
remembered that Tuesday in November 1856 when she and her
younger sister Mary stood by the window of Forest Home and
watched their brother Oliver ride off with their father to cast his
first ballot for Republican presidential candidate John C.
Fremont.

A lump rose in her throat, she felt a strange ache in her heart,
and tears blurred her eyes. She turned to Mary, and "she, dear
little innocent, seemed wonderfully sober, too."

"Wouldn't you like to vote as well as Oliver? Don't you and I
love the country just as well as he, and doesn't the country need
our ballots?" Frank asked.

Mary, a bit scared, replied, " 'Course we do, and 'course we ought,—but don't you go ahead and say so, for then we would be called strong-minded."

Frances Elizabeth Caroline Willard (1839–98) was never afraid of being labeled strong-minded, but epithets were seldom used to describe her. Instead she became the nineteenth century's most beloved and respected female leader, the only woman to be enshrined in the United States Capitol's Statuary Hall. Her life epitomizes the twisted strand of women's history in the nineteenth century.

Born 28 September 1839 in Churchville, New York, Frances was heir to a distinguished New England heritage. Two Willards served as early presidents of Harvard University. One of them, Samuel, as pastor of Old South Church in Boston, opposed the burning of witches. Her mother, Mary Thompson Hill (1805–92), was born in Danville, Vermont. Josiah Flint Willard (1805–68) was born in Wheelock, Vermont. Both families migrated from Vermont to New York's Genesee Valley when the children were about ten. Mary and Josiah were married on 3 November 1831. Both had been successful teachers. Josiah managed a local store.

In her autobiography, *Glimpses of Fifty Years,* Willard says that in 1829 her father announced his intention to become a Christian. After several days he did "pray through." She attributes to him the revival that swept their community, resulting in the conversion of thirty heads of families along with many young people. Churchville, however, was only fourteen miles west of Rochester, the heart of the "burned-over district." Charles Grandison Finney had been stirring the area with revivals since 1826. His work culminated with the great Rochester revival of 1830.

Josiah and Mary became leading members of a "union church," known simply as "The Church of God in Ogden" or the "old Stone Church," built in 1832 by a congregation of Presbyterians, Baptists, Methodists, and even Unitarians.

OBERLIN

In the autumn of 1841 the Willard family decided to migrate to Finney's fledgling school, Oberlin Collegiate Institute in

Ohio. They did so for a variety of reasons. They were influenced, according to Frances, by a young graduate of Hamilton College and probably a Finney convert during his Utica revival of 1825–26, who boarded with the Willards while teaching in Churchville and saving money to become a minister. Josiah also felt called to the ministry. Oberlin was the first college to admit both men and women, so Mary and her sister Sarah Hill would take classes too. Finally, the Willards wanted to associate with Oberlin because of its stand on abolition, in which both firmly believed. Their cellar in Oberlin became a haven for travelers on the Underground Railroad, and Frances learned to read from *The Slave's Friend,* an abolitionist magazine for children.

Josiah enrolled in the collegiate course. Mary, after the birth of their daughter Mary in 1843, took courses in moral philosophy and religion. She also became involved in Lydia Andrews Finney's "moral improvement" group. Both Willards joined Finney's First Congregational Church. Though Frances was only a child, she retained vivid memories of their five years in Ohio: hearing the thunder of Finney's voice and seeing the lightning of his great light eyes, meeting Lucy Stone, mimicking the cadence and gestures of students practicing rhetoric.

However, in 1845 Josiah suffered hemorrhaging in his lungs, and the family decided to move to the wide open spaces of Wisconsin, where it was hoped the fresh air and manual labor of farming would improve his health. There Frances grew to womanhood at Forest Home.

Before long she was writing all the time, editing a newspaper for the family, keeping a journal, and composing stories. Concerned about their children's schooling, the Willards organized a local one-room school in 1854. The teacher had been a classics tutor at Oberlin. When Oliver went off to the Methodists' Beloit College in 1852, Frances begged him to bring home books for her to read. When Aunt Sarah Hill came to teach history at the Milwaukee Female College, Frances was enrolled there in 1857. The next year the whole Willard family moved to Evanston so the girls could enroll at the Methodists' new Northwestern Female College.

Since the Methodist circuit rider was the only organizer of religion in the wilds of Wisconsin, the Willards had changed allegiances. The faith commitment was to be a deep one for Frances. She was scheduled to give the valedictory address at Northwestern in June 1859, but a bout of typhoid fever laid her low. During the fearful illness, she experienced conversion. She later described it as a contest between two presences: "One presence was to me warm, sunny, safe, with an impression as of snowy wings; the other cold, dismal, dark, with the flutter of a bat." Eventually she responded, "If God lets me get well I'll try to be a Christian girl." The next winter she affirmed her faith during revival services at First Methodist Church. She became a full member on 5 May 1861, "an active worker, seeking to lead others to Christ."

In 1866 the noted holiness evangelists "Dr. and Mrs. Phoebe Palmer" spoke at First Methodist. Under their ministry Willard experienced the "second blessing," holiness, or entire sanctification. While the memory of the experience would last a lifetime, possession of it would not. Having taught for several years in schools around Chicago, she accepted a position at Genesee Wesleyan Seminary in Lima, New York. Since the Genesee Conference had been wracked with division—first the controversy over abolition in 1844 which resulted in Orange Scott's formation of the Free Methodist Church, and then the holiness controversy in 1860 which spawned B. T. Roberts's and Luther Lee's Wesleyan Methodist Connection—men advised her to keep quiet about her beliefs, despite the Palmers' clear teaching that testimony to the experience was requisite for its retention. Willard kept quiet and lost the consciousness of her experience.

In 1868 Kate A. Jackson, with whom Frances had lived and taught for several years, suggested a trip to Europe, to be financed by Kate's father. The grand tour, from May 1868 to September 1870, greatly expanded the horizons of the farm girl from Wisconsin—from the British Isles, to the Continent, to Egypt and Palestine. She admits in her autobiography that on the advice of a physician she avoided the water and drank local beer and wine.

COLLEGE PRESIDENT

Upon her return to Evanston in the fall of 1870, Willard was asked to become president of the newly founded Evanston

College for Ladies, which had absorbed the assets of her alma mater. Since she had helped the American Methodist Ladies Centenary Association raise $30,000 in 1865–66 to build Heck Hall at Garrett Biblical Institute, the college's sponsors had confidence that she could build their school. So she pre-empted Chicago's 1871 Fourth of July celebration, luring ten thousand people to Evanston for a celebration, cornerstone-laying, and pledge solicitation. The school opened that fall, and the next spring Frances Willard became the first woman college president in America to confer degrees.

But the triumph was short-lived. The Chicago fire destroyed the resources of many who had pledged support. The college merged with Northwestern University, and Willard became dean of the Woman's College and professor of aesthetics on the liberal arts faculty. Initially Northwestern was under the presidency of E. O. Haven, who pledged that "every door should be flung wide to humanity's gentler half," but the new president was Charles Fowler, to whom Willard was briefly engaged in 1861. She broke the engagement, and he forever carried a grudge. At Northwestern he began to undermine her authority with the women students. On 13 June 1874 she resigned. As she later explained to D. L. Moody: "Dr. Fowler has the will of a Napoleon, I have the will of a Queen Elizabeth; when an immovable meets an indestructible object, something has to give way."

Disillusioned with academe and casting about for new direction, Willard heard about the Crusade against intemperance which sprang up during the winter of 1873–74 in southern Ohio and upstate New York. "The pentecost of God fell on them in those fifty days of the Crusade," she said later. Her mother became one of the founders of the Evanston temperance society, and Frances became its delegate to the first national convention of the Woman's Christian Temperance Union (WCTU) in Cleveland that fall. Since she had contacts with Methodist women across the country, she was elected corresponding secretary.

As a child, she had cut the following pledge from a magazine, pasted it in the family Bible, and insisted that every member of the family sign his or her name to it:

A pledge we make, no wine to take,
Nor brandy red that turns the head,
Nor fiery rum that ruins home,
Nor whiskey hot that makes the sot,
Nor brewers' beer, for that we fear,
And cider, too, will never do;
To quench our thirst we'll always bring
Cold water from the well or spring.
So here we pledge perpetual hate,
To all that can intoxicate.

Now she threw herself into the work: writing, corresponding, speaking, traveling, organizing. Her constant prayer was, "What wouldst thou have me to do?"

THE "WOMAN QUESTION"

Then, declared Willard in *Glimpses of Fifty Years,* "while alone on my knees one Sabbath in the capital of the Crusade State"—Columbus, Ohio—"in May of the centennial year"—1876—in the home of a "veteran Crusader,"

there was borne in upon my mind, as I believe, from loftier regions, the declaration, "You are to speak for woman's ballot as a weapon of protection to her home and tempted loved ones from the tyranny of drink," and then for the first and only time in my life, there flashed through my brain a complete line of argument and illustration. . . .

Willard had inherited an interest in suffrage from her mother's breast. As a child she had met Lucy Stone, who now headed the American Woman Suffrage Association and edited the *Woman's Journal.* She had met Elizabeth Cady Stanton and Susan B. Anthony, leaders of the National Woman Suffrage Association. But she had held aloof from the movement in the 1860s and early 1870s because, as biographer Ray (Rachel) Strachey notes, "suffrage was too advanced and radical a thing, connected in those days with too much ridicule and scorn, a thing unwomanly and unscriptural, and to touch it was contamination."

The woman question had certainly been raised for Willard

in Europe. She had written in her diary, "What can be done to make the world a wider place for women?" In Paris she decided to study the issue and speak out against what she termed "unenlightened public opinion." Her first public lecture, given upon her return from Europe, was entitled "The New Chivalry." In it she discussed the degradation of women throughout the world.

While she always portrays her adoption of the suffrage issue as a conversion experience, she acknowledges in *Woman and Temperance* that women had already passed through the states of "petition work, local-option work, and constitutional-prohibition-amendment work," and she had become convinced that women must have the ballot as a "home protection" weapon. Thus after her conversion, she immediately wrote WCTU president Annie Wittenmyer, a Methodist laywoman, and asked permission to speak on the subject at a centennial international temperance convention scheduled for Philadelphia. Wittenmyer refused. Willard wanted to speak on the theme at Chautauqua where she had been told "our platform is free to those whom we invite," but she felt the leader's "preference so strongly" that she "refrained from speaking out my deepest thought." Finally she went to the holiness campground, Old Orchard Beach, Maine, and there she spoke first of her "pet heresy" and "avowed the faith that was within."

When she arrived at the WCTU's third annual convention in Newark, New Jersey, in late October 1876, she felt in her soul that "woe is me if I declare not this gospel." Thus, "welcome or not," she decided, "the words must come." At the close of her speech, a Presbyterian woman from Syracuse who was chairing the meeting hastened to make it clear that "the speaker represents herself and not the Woman's Christian Temperance Union, for we do not propose to trail our skirts through the mire of politics." As they left the hall, Mrs. Wittenmyer whispered, "You might have been a leader, but now you'll be only a scout."

Willard admitted that she "could but feel the strong conservatism of an audience of Christian women," yet she "felt far more strongly the undergirdings of the Spirit." And evidently the Spirit was moving in that audience of conservative churchwomen. Following the speech, Hannah Whitall Smith

(1832–1911), already famous for *The Christian's Secret of a Happy Life* and destined to be one of Willard's staunchest co-workers and most loyal friends, found an older woman sobbing bitterly. Trying to comfort her, Smith asked the cause of her tears. She replied, "Frances Willard has just convinced me that I ought to want to vote, and I *don't want to!"*

THE WORK OF AN EVANGELIST

Reaction was so strong that for a year Willard more or less dropped out of national temperance work. In February 1877 she joined revivalist D. L. Moody for meetings in Boston. For three months she spoke every afternoon on some biblical text at either the Berkeley Street or Park Street Congregational church. She was also invited to speak in the surrounding suburbs as well as to a "congregation of women" on Sunday evenings at Clarendon Street Baptist Church. In *Glimpses of Fifty Years* she notes that Moody even asked her to preach one Sunday afternoon.

"Brother Moody, you need not think because I am a Western woman and not afraid to go, you must put me in the forefront of the battle after this fashion. Perhaps you will hinder the work among these conservatives," Frances suggested. Moody only laughed and told her "it was just what they needed" and that she "need n't be scared for he was n't."

Actually Willard always nursed a secret call to ministry and eventually defended women's ministry in her 1888 book, *Woman in the Pulpit.* She wrote Moody—through his wife Emma Revell—concerning her thoughts on women and the church:

> All my life I have been devoted to the advancement of women in education and opportunity. I firmly believe God has a work for them to do as evangelists, as bearers of Christ's message to the ungospeled, to the prayer-meeting, to the church generally and the world at large, such as most people have not dreamed. It is therefore my dearest wish to help break down the barriers of prejudice that keep them silent. I cannot think that meetings in which "the brethren" only are called upon, are one half as effective as those where all are freely invited, and I can but believe that "women's meetings," as such, are a relic of an

outworn *régime*. Never did I hold one of these meetings without a protest in my soul against it. As in the day of Pentecost, so now, let men and women in perfectly impartial fashion participate in all services conducted in His name in whom there is neither bond nor free, male nor female, but all are one.

While her soul may have protested holding "women's meetings," she actually resigned from Moody's team because of his complaints about her sharing the platform at a temperance convention with Mary Rice Livermore (1820–1905), wife of a Universalist minister, committed suffragist, and temperance leader. Echoing John Wesley's "if thy heart be as my heart, give me thy hand" and "think and let think," Willard wrote Emma Moody:

For myself, the more I study the subject, the more I fail to see that it is for us to decide who shall work in this cause side by side with us, and who shall not. I cannot judge how the hearts of earnest, pure, prayerful women may appear in God's clear sight, nor just when their loyalty to Christ has reached the necessary degree.

In Boston that winter, Frances acquired her life's companion, Anna Gordon (1853–1931). "Nanny" was a talented musician, and, as Willard's devoted secretary, she became a very capable manager, organizer, and speaker, especially with children. After Willard's death she became her biographer and legend-maker.

Back home in Evanston, Willard was elected president of the Illinois WCTU and embarked on a home protection campaign to secure the right of women to vote on temperance issues in local elections. Within three months the women of Illinois collected 180,000 signatures on petitions headed with a slogan which Willard had coined and which was to become the WCTU watchword: For God and Home and Native Land. Petitions in hand, the women marched on Springfield. They sang "Home, Sweet Home" in the senate and prayed in committee rooms. Though their efforts were in vain (at least for that session—the bill did eventually pass), they learned the realities of politics firsthand.

With the Illinois experience as a case in point, Willard went to the national WCTU convention in Baltimore in 1878 to argue for the home protection ballot again. Opposition was stiff. A local woman informed her that on the East Coast the issue was still a "green persimmon." Replied Willard: "This Home Protection petition is a green persimmon in Maryland, but, my friends, it is a ripe one yonder on the prairies." Despite her plea, the convention voted 43–42 not to get involved with suffrage.

WCTU PRESIDENT

However, Willard arrived at the 1879 national convention in Indianapolis as the avowed leader of a liberal wing of the WCTU and proceeded to unseat Wittenmyer as president. She was to serve in the office until her death in 1898. The organization she took control of in 1879 was already the largest women's group in the United States and probably in the world, but within the next ten years its membership would quadruple. She completely reorganized the structure of the WCTU and nurtured it into not only the largest, but also the most efficient and effective women's organization in the nineteenth century. It was in the WCTU that the leadership was trained that gave birth to the Nineteenth Amendment in 1920.

As she became more and more a public figure, Willard tried to maintain ties with the Methodist Episcopal Church—though the church did not make it easy. As president of the WCTU, many of whose members were Methodists, she visited the General Conference of 1880 meeting in Cincinnati to bring greetings and to solicit the church's support. To use a modern phrase, it was a consciousness-raising experience. The conference was already embattled over women's issues because Anna Howard Shaw and Anna Oliver had asked for full ordination in addition to their local preachers' licenses. Friends of Willard introduced a motion to give her ten minutes in which to speak. The motion evoked more than two hours of acrimonious debate. When the vote was finally taken, two-thirds of the delegates favored her speaking, but her chief opponent vowed to "exhaust parliamentary resources to prevent it." Willard decided to simply leave the assembly a gracious note and depart. Shaw (1847–1919), who was a lifelong friend and colleague of Willard's and who eventually became president of the National American Woman Suffrage Association (NAWSA), was ordained by the Methodist Protestants. The Methodist Episcopal Church denied ordination to Oliver and even went so far as to withdraw all preaching licenses from women.

Awakened to the plight of women in church assemblies, Willard could not resist noting in her first presidential address that fall in Boston that "two-thirds of Christ's church are women, whose persuasive voices will be a reinforcement quite indispensable to the evangelizing agencies of the more hopeful future." She also quoted Finney: "The church that silences the women is shorn of half its power."

Willard was back at the Methodist General Conference in 1888 in New York City, this time as one of the first five duly elected female local lay delegates. After another lengthy and vicious debate, this time led by her rejected suitor, now bishop, Charles Fowler, the women were denied seats. Willard was so angry and disappointed that in her presidential address that year, delivered from the same platform, she threatened to withdraw from the Methodist church and found her own.

Willard's goal, as had been Finney's, was "the Christianizing of society." Through temperance, she sought to engineer alliances not only with the church but with a host of political and labor organizations. She called it gospel politics. She first formed a national coalition called the Home Protection Party in 1881, seeking to unite the efforts of the Prohibition Party with those of the WCTU. In response to the WCTU's support, the Prohibition Party supported woman's rights. She also endorsed the Knights of Labor in return for their support of temperance and suffrage. After the Prohibition Party's poor showing in the 1888 elections, Willard plunged into the maelstrom of farmer's alliances, labor groups, and black organizations. She summoned leaders to Chicago to formulate what she called a people's party, from which the Populist Party eventually emerged. However, its platform was quite different from what Willard proposed. She could deliver no votes, and so women's issues were ignored. But her "do-everything policy" went far beyond politics. In 1889, for example, the Chicago WCTU alone was sponsoring two day nurseries, two Sunday schools, an industrial school, a mission to shelter four thousand destitute or homeless women per year, a free medical dispensary which treated sixteen hundred people that year, a lodging house for men, and a low-cost restaurant. The national WCTU had forty departments of activities.

Willard's last major effort was to make temperance, the growing drug traffic, and women's issues international concerns. In 1884 the WCTU commissioned a missionary, Mary Clement Leavitt, who set forth on what proved to be a nine-year around-the-world journey with the "Polyglot Petition," seeking to unite women and men of all nations against the drug and liquor traffic. The first convention of the world WCTU was held in 1891 with representatives from forty countries. Willard was named its president as well, Anna Gordon its assistant secretary. Willard was to preside at its first four biennial conventions (the last in 1897, when membership stood at more than two million women around the globe).

At the World's Woman's Christian Temperance Union organizing convention, Frances was introduced to Lady Henry Somerset. Hurt by a disastrous marriage which ended after ten years in a scandalous divorce, Lady Henry had been touched in her loneliness by a humble band of Methodists in the village near her castle. About the same time she met and became friends with Hannah Whitall Smith, who had recently taken up residence in England. It was Smith who nominated Lady Henry as president of the British WCTU and accompanied her to America to meet Frances Willard. Their attraction for each other was immediate and intense. Grieved by her mother's recent death and wearied by tensions within the WCTU over the building of the Temple in Chicago to house its headquarters, Willard spent much of her remaining time in England at Lady Henry's several estates.

In 1897 she returned to the United States for the WCTU national convention and to make a pilgrimage to her life scenes: the birthplaces of her parents in Vermont, Churchville to see Aunt Sarah, Oberlin to visit her childhood home, and on to Evanston, and Janesville, Wisconsin. Then she went back east, hoping to sail for England again.

Instead she died on 17 February 1898 at age fifty-eight in New York City with Anna Gordon at her side. Services were held in

Finney's old Broadway Tabernacle. Her body was taken by train through Churchville, then to Chicago for viewing at the Temple. Twenty thousand people lined the winter streets to bid farewell. Thousands more waited in the slush and snow of Evanston. Final services were held 23 February at First Methodist Church. Her body was buried with those of her family in Rose Hill Cemetery. Willard had asked to be cremated. Though Gordon bridled at the request, she finally conceded to her beloved companion's wishes. The body was removed from its vault, and on Easter morning, 9 April 1898, Willard's body was cremated and her ashes deposited in her mother's casket.

She was indeed "Woman of the Century." Heir to the revivalist legacy of broad-based, gospel-rooted reform, Willard sought to do everything within her power to empower and uplift women. Gathering up all the strands of women's resources and efforts, she brought together in one huge, very political organization the power to make women a force in American life.

CHAPTER 2

THE WHOLE AGE
MUST COOPERATE

*In order to be developed, an idea must be in
harmony with surrounding civilization, and the
whole age must cooperate with it.*

—*Taine*

For America the nineteenth century was a time of
incredible expansion, change, upheaval, and progress. From an
essentially agrarian cluster of states perched on the edge of a
continent at the frontier of the Western world, America spread
to fill a continent full of cities, factories, and multinational
monopolies, an imperial nation with aspirations of world
leadership. Many saw "the upward-tending spirit of the age,
busy in a hundred forms of effort for the world's redemption
from the sins and sufferings which oppress it" as the dawning of
God's millennial glory.

In 1800 upstate New York and Kentucky *were* the frontier.
Only sixteen states were united. The Northwest Territory
produced Ohio in 1803, Indiana in 1816, and Illinois in 1818.
The Louisiana Purchase of 1803 added Louisiana in 1812.
Gold lured many across the continent, and California became
a state in 1850. Bloody Kansas was admitted to the Union in
1861; Colorado in 1876. By the time Wyoming became a state
in 1890, women were allowed to vote on the issue. Historian
Frederick Jackson Turner has argued that this continuous
vision of open land gave to American society its incredible
expansiveness and optimism. Having warred and won with
Great Britain (1812), Mexico (1848), and Spain (1898),
America was ready to extend its Manifest Destiny to
encompass the world.

The ever-expanding frontier created a vacuum to be filled

MIGRANTS AND IMMIGRANTS

with people, migrants from the eastern seaboard and immigrants from around the world. In colonial New England, families expected to divide their land among their sons, but as families continued generation after generation, only eldest sons could find enough land; younger sons searched westward for more land, cheaper land, more fertile land. They became a river flowing from Connecticut to upstate New York, down the Ohio Valley, across Indiana, Illinois, and into Kansas. From there the little houses fanned out across the prairie.

Laura Ingalls Wilder (1867–1957) chronicled her own family's movements. Pa, Charles Ingalls, was born during "The Big Snow" of January 1836 in upstate Allegany County, New York. His parents' roots were in New Hampshire and Vermont. "Westward the course of Empire takes its way," they said, and the Ingalls family joined the migration to the prairies of Illinois, to "Skunk City," Chicago, and then on into "The Big Woods" of Wisconsin. Laura's Ma, Caroline Quiner, was born 2 December 1839 in Milwaukee County, to a family of Connecticut Yankees. Charles Ingalls and Caroline Quiner were married 1 February 1860 in Concord, Jefferson County, Wisconsin. The family moved west to Pipin County on the Mississippi River. There Laura was born. Soon she too was caught up in migration—to Missouri and Kansas, to Burr Oak, Iowa, and Walnut Grove, Minnesota; to De Smet, South Dakota, and finally to Rocky Ridge Farm in Mansfield, Missouri, with her husband, Almanzo Wilder, a farm boy from Malone, New York.

The already-American migrants were joined by the immigrants. The English and Scottish Presbyterians continued to come to New York, New Jersey, the Carolinas. The Lutheran and Roman Catholic Germans both settled in Cincinnati, St. Louis, and Milwaukee. The Swedes, Norwegians, Danes, and Finns farmed the prairies of Minnesota, the Dakotas, and Nebraska. Compelled by the potato famine of 1846 and 1847, the Roman Catholic Irish provided factory workers and domestics for Boston and New York. Between 1815 and 1860, 5.5 million immigrants arrived in the United States, two-thirds of them through the port of New York. By 1850 nearly half the city's population was foreign-born, glutting the labor market and stirring social concern among the city's leaders.

And then there were the others. Between 1860 and 1900 another 14 million immigrants came. Chinese to pan California's gold and build the railroads. Beginning in the 1870s, the flood of Eastern and Southern Europeans—Austrians and Hungarians, Bohemians, Serbs, Poles, Italians, and Russians. They came not for land in the West but to the cities, the factories, the ethnic neighborhoods. Said Jacob Riis of New York City in 1890:

> A map of the city, colored to designate nationalities, would show more stripes than on the skin of a zebra, and more colors than any rainbow. The city on such a map would fall into two great halves, green for the Irish prevailing in the West Side tenement districts, and blue for the Germans on the East Side. But intermingled with these ground colors would be an odd variety of tinges that would give the whole the appearance of an extraordinary crazy-quilt.

It was indeed a wondrous sight for those born when Greenwich Village was still a village, beyond the outskirts of New York.

The census of 1810 counted 7.25 million Americans; the census takers of 1860 found 31.4 million; by 1900, nearly 76 million. In colonial days men outnumbered women, but the men moved westward, and by 1840 women were in the majority in the East.

AN AGE OF INVENTION

Americans fanned out across the country by increasingly rapid modes of transportation. Fearing sectionalism, Henry Clay and John C. Calhoun proposed in 1817 a national system of roads and canals. In the 1820s and 1830s steamboats plied the Ohio and Mississippi rivers. Keelboats made the round trip from Cincinnati to New Orleans in seventy-eight days; steamboats reduced that time to thirty. Yankee clippers took American goods around the world and brought home raw materials and treasures. Conestoga wagons traveled the

National, the Cumberland Road from Baltimore to Wheeling, West Virginia, and on to Vandalia, Illinois. In 1817 New York began to build the Erie Canal. In 1825, on the eve of Finney's revivals, Clinton's Ditch opened to traffic the 363 miles from New York City to Lake Erie. Ohio linked the Great Lakes to the Mississippi Valley by canal in 1834. Other states developed similar canal systems.

At the same time the first horse-drawn railroad presaged the demise of canals. Soon the Baltimore and Ohio was in operation, to be followed at midcentury by the New York Central and the Pennsylvania railroads. In 1848 Illinois had no railroad tracks; by 1855 ten trunk lines and eleven branches carried ninety-six trains, making Chicago the rail hub of the nation. The Oregon Trail became part of the Central Pacific and the Union Pacific railways, which were completed in 1869. In 1865 only 35,000 miles of railroad were in operation; by 1900 the figure was just under 200,000 miles—a vast network of high-speed, economical transportation for farm products, industrial output, and people.

The railroads not only linked the vast farmlands to the waterways, they also connected the burgeoning cities. In 1800 only five cities housed more than 10,000: New York, Philadelphia, Baltimore, Charleston, and Boston. In 1810 only forty-six communities were designated "urban," having a population of more than 2,500! By 1860 there were 393, with New York and Philadelphia each housing more than half a million. By 1830 a quarter of America's population lived beyond the Appalachians. In 1840 Cincinnati had a population of 46,000 who called it the Queen City of the West; British traveler Harriet Martineau dubbed it "Porkopolis." St. Louis, the Gateway to the West, had only 16,000 people in 1840 but 77,000 in 1850. Fort Dearborn, established in 1803, was incorporated as Chicago in 1837, and the Second City had 1.5 million inhabitants by the end of the century. Marshall Field and Montgomery Ward in the 1870s and Sears in the 1880s made it the center of mass merchandising. By 1880 nineteen cities had more than 100,000 people; by 1900 that number had become thirty-six. The population of New York City was 3.5 million.

The nation was increasingly knit together by lines of

communication. Samuel Morse had little inkling of "what hath God wrought!" when he telegraphed that message from Washington to Baltimore in 1844. Western Union was organized in 1856, and its lines were credited with spreading the 1857–58 holiness revival across the nation. A decade and a half of efforts culminated in 1866 with the laying of the first transatlantic cable, and communication from the Continent became a matter of seconds instead of days. Highlight of the 1876 Philadelphia Exposition was Alexander Graham Bell's newest toy, the telephone.

Every city needed a hotel, a newspaper, and a college. Hotels were an American invention, "palaces of the public," testing laboratories for conveniences such as steam heat, elevators, gas lights, spring beds, and indoor plumbing. Tenements for the poor reached six stories before the widespread use of indoor facilities. Chicago had no plumbing before the Civil War. Sewage and garbage disposal were obvious problems, with their concomitants: impure water and vermin, disease and epidemic—tuberculosis (consumption), diptheria, cholera, puerperal fever. Immigration and economic fluctuation led to poverty, prostitution, drinking, and family violence. Urban government developed of necessity, and private charity was stretched beyond its limits. Crime statistics sometimes justified references to the "vicious poor."

A NATION OF INDUSTRY

In 1800 America was an agrarian nation; in 1900 it was not. Jefferson's "great agrarian democracy" had become the most highly industrialized nation on earth. Moving westward, the nation discovered and came to appreciate its vast natural resources: iron ore, coal, natural gas, copper, gold, silver, and oil. The immigrants provided the necessary labor. Yankee ingenuity invented a new world. The United States Patent Office was created in 1790. By 1860 it had granted 36,000 patents; between 1860 and 1890 another 440,000 were issued. They included the electromagnet, the electric motor, the dynamo, and the transformer; the revolving pistol; the process for vulcanizing rubber, and the sewing machine. Business discovered the typewriter, the cash register, and the adding machine. The linotype composing machine fostered the growth of newspapers, books, periodicals, and pamphlets. Farm production was multiplied by the chilled plow, the twine binder, the reaper, and the threshing machine. Hotels, restaurants, and commercial laundries used improved gas stoves, gas refrigerators, electric suction vacuum cleaners, mechanical dishwashers, and steam washing machines, but it would be the 1920s before these would be reduced to household size.

Iron ore had been mined from colonial days and manufactured around eastern Pennsylvania and northern New Jersey. In the 1840s the industry moved west to Pittsburgh, and then giant deposits were found in the Marquette area of northern Michigan and the Mesabi range at the head of Lake Superior. The steel industry moved to Cleveland, Toledo, Gary, Chicago, and Milwaukee where the ore boats met the railroad cars of coal. In the 1870s the Bessemer process came into use, and then the open hearth. It was a dirty business. Rebecca Harding Davis described "Life in the Iron Mills" of Wheeling, West Virginia, for readers of the April 1861 *Atlantic Monthly:*

> The idiosyncrasy of this town is smoke. It rolls sullenly in slow folds from the great chimneys of the iron-foundries, and settles down in black, slimy pools on the muddy streets. . . . The long train of mules, dragging masses of pig-iron through the narrow street, have a foul vapor hanging to their reeking sides.
> . . . [F]rom the street-window I look on the slow stream of human life creeping past, night and morning, to the great mills. Masses of men, with dull, besotted faces bent to the ground, sharpened here and there by pain or cunning; skin and muscle and flesh begrimed with smoke and ashes; stooping all night over boiling caldrons of metal, laired by day in dens of drunkenness and infamy; breathing from infancy to death an air saturated with fog and grease and soot, vileness for soul and body.

Industrialization had begun quietly. First a few textile factories, powered by New England's rivers, employed young women prior to their anticipated marriages. Built on the domestic system of labor then practiced, the factories were often owned by a kin network and sometimes hired whole families, particularly those of widows. By 1840 New England had twelve hundred cotton factories and by 1850 another fifteen hundred woolen mills. Sawmills and gristmills, tanneries and fulling mills sprang up. Rochester, New York, was one of the fastest-growing communities in the country in the 1820s. At the junction of the Erie Canal and the Genesee River, Rochester was laid out in 1812 as the perfect mill site, powered by a two-hundred-foot water fall. The Erie Canal reached there in 1821. When the canal was finished to New York City in 1823, the valley became one of the greatest grain-growing regions of the world. In 1818, Rochester had exported 26,000 barrels of flour, in 1828, 200,000 barrels; and by 1838 half a million barrels were produced annually. The city became the center of a market economy with the commercialization of agriculture. And manufacturing was beginning. With Charles Finney's extraordinary revival there in the winter of 1830–31, it also became the center of religious enthusiasm and reform.

In the 1840s and 1850s, a major shift occurred. The domestic economy of skilled artisans and small merchants surrounded by family and apprentices gave way to the factory system entirely, with business and factory in one location, workers living in boarding houses, the owner's home located elsewhere with wife and children securely lodged there, and the owner/husband/father shuttling daily between.

After the Civil War fierce competition resulted in pools, declared illegal by the Interstate Commerce Act in 1887. Business simply reorganized into trusts. Standard Oil Company, organized by John D. Rockefeller in 1870, was reorganized as a trust in 1882. Andrew Carnegie's United States Steel, the American Sugar Refining Company, the American Tobacco Company, International Harvester, the Pullman Palace Car Company, the railroads, and finally in 1900 American Telephone and Telegraph remapped American industry. They brought an end to local industry, the locally self-sufficient community. Not until the 1870s and 1880s did labor begin to gather its forces. Before the war there had been a tolerable mix of comfortable middle class and surviving poor; after the war society was polarized between the incredibly wealthy robber barons and the wretchedly poor.

THE BODY POLITIC

In politics the country was also on the move. The election of 1800 was the first to witness the divisiveness of the two-party system. Thomas Jefferson defeated Federalist John Adams, and was reelected in 1804. For religious people party politics represented a sure sign of self-interest and a lack of true godliness. For politicians it was a tug of war between centralizing national forces and decentralizing sectional forces. The Age of the Common Man began with the election of Andrew Jackson in 1828. The change had come gradually with the disestablishment of the churches—the Episcopal church in Virginia in 1785, and the Congregational church in Connecticut (1818), New Hampshire (1819), and Massachusetts (1833). The standing order was giving way. State constitutions were revised in the 1820s to grant "universal manhood suffrage," without religious or property qualification.

In 1840, as the issue of slavery began to rend the country, the Democrats and Whigs were joined in battle by the abolitionists' Liberty Party, and then in 1848 by the Free Soil Party. Its motto was Free trade, free labor, free soil, free speech, free men. The first Republican candidate was John C. Fremont in 1856. The Prohibition Party fielded its first candidate in 1872, as did the Greenback Party. The East, Midwest, and West were being tied together; the South was drifting away. The North was surging toward the twentieth century; the lower South still lived in the eighteenth. There, until the war, slaves and cotton preserved a structured, agrarian, aristocratic culture.

Although Congress had outlawed traffic in slaves in 1807, black Africans continued to be imported into the southern states via Cuba. In 1833 slavery was abolished in Great Britain, and American critics adopted the slogan, "Immediate abolition." The Missouri Compromise of 1820 had maintained the balance of slave and free states established by the Mason-Dixon line in 1819. It admitted Missouri as slave and Maine as free but did not end debate on the admission of future states. The Compromise of 1850 abolished slavery in Washington, D.C., and admitted California as a free state but left New Mexico and Utah to popular sovereignty and included the Fugitive Slave Law.

With the Kansas-Nebraska Act of 1854 and the Dred Scott decision of 1857, compromise began to unravel. Four years of conflagration resulted. The Thirteenth Amendment (1865) prohibited slavery, the Fourteenth (1868) guaranteed due process and equal protection, and the Fifteenth (1870) gave black *males* the right to vote. The slaves were emancipated, but the women who had worked so long in their behalf, as well as that half of the slaves who were women, were asked to step back to let the black man step forward.

Political debates were fueled by fires other than abolition as well. America has always been prone to various forms of national paranoia, the conspiracy mentality. The first fanaticism which hit New York's burned-over district in the 1820s was directed against Masons. The disturbance began in 1826 with the unexplained disappearance of William Morgan from Batavia, New York. Before he could publish a book revealing secret Masonic rituals, he was allegedly deposited on the bottom of the Niagara River. In the early 1830s an Anti-Masonic Party drew support from Maine to the Western Reserve.

Immigrants, especially the Roman Catholics, were another continuing source of paranoia. In 1834 a Charlestown, Massachusetts, mob burned the local Ursuline convent school after Congregational clergyman Lyman Beecher delivered three violently anti-Catholic sermons. His *Plea for the West* (1835) warned of possible Roman Catholic domination in the Mississippi Valley if Protestants did not evangelize. The fires were fueled by Rebecca Reed's *Six Months in a Convent* and Maria Monk's *Awful Disclosures of the Hotel Dieu Nunnery of Montreal,* both of which appeared in 1836. The Native American Party emerged in 1844. It evolved into the Know-Nothing Party, which flourished in the 1850s. Many assumed that what was wrong with America was the fault of others: Masons, slaveholders, the liquor interests, the ignorant, the papists.

THE BENEVOLENCE EMPIRE

However, suspicion of one's neighbors was also mixed with concern and caring. The first half of the nineteenth century saw the phenomenal rise of the Benevolence Empire. Based largely on the voluntary work and fund raising of women, society moved from philanthropy into reform and on to social work—and back again. The movement is usually dated from 1797 when a Scottish Presbyterian widow, Isabella Graham, founded the Society for the Relief of Poor Widows with Small Children, which eventually became the New York Orphan Asylum. She and her daughter Joanna Graham Bethune are better known for founding Sunday schools, initially to provide basic education to working children, poor children, black children. In 1824, Joanna and Divy Bethune founded the American Sunday School Union.

The empire grew rapidly to include the American Board of Commissioners for Foreign Missions (1810), American Bible Society (1816), American Colonization Society (1817), American Tract Society (1825), American Education Society (1826), American Home Mission Society (1826), American Temperance Society (1826), American Peace Society (1828), and American Anti-Slavery Society (1833). Beyond these major organizations were a variety of other concerns, often led by women: concerns for the handicapped, the imprisoned, the mentally ill, the poor. As women began to speak out on behalf of others, they found power and reason to speak out on their own behalf. They also experimented with a total spectrum of strategies from religious conversion and moral suasion to petition and political party to job retraining and relocation to sociological investigation and government legislation.

It was an age of ultra-isms. Beyond the reformers were those who would remake society. Religious communitarians built such places as Ephrata, Pennsylvania; Zoar, Ohio; Bishop Hill, Illinois; and Amana, Iowa. Mother Ann Lee's Shakers founded a number of settlements. Out of transcendentalism arose Hopedale and Brook Farm. Perfectionist John Humphrey Noyes founded the Oneida Community to practice Bible communism and complex marriage. From a more utopian socialism grew Robert Owen's New Harmony, Frances Wright's Nashoba, and the Fourierist phalanxes. Most successful and durable was Joseph Smith's Church of Jesus Christ of Latter-day Saints, the Mormons. Founded in the burned-over district, they moved to Ohio, Missouri, and

Nauvoo, Ilinois. After Smith's murder there in 1844, they moved to the state of Deseret, to build Zion in the wilderness of Utah.

A TRULY AMERICAN CULTURE

In the nineteenth century the young nation found time at last to develop a national culture, both high and popular. The Literature books still anthologize Ralph Waldo Emerson and Henry David Thoreau, Nathaniel Hawthorne and Herman Melville, Walt Whitman and Emily Dickinson, Edgar Allan Poe and O. Henry, Mark Twain and Upton Sinclair. More popular in their day were such "scribbling women" as Fanny Fern (Sara Payson Willis) Fanny Forester (Emily Chubbuck Judson), Grace Greenwood (Sara Jane Clarke Lippincott), Josiah Allen's Wife (Marietta Holley), and Susan Warner. The book of the century was, of course, the book which caused the war: Harriet Beecher Stowe's *Uncle Tom's Cabin.* Like her sister-authors, Harriet, younger daughter of revivalist Lyman Beecher, and wife of Calvin Stowe, a professor at Lane Seminary, wrote to support her family and to supply the burgeoning "penny press," such magazines as the Methodist *Ladies' Repository* and Sarah Josepha Hale's *Godey's Lady's Book,* and the newly mechanized printing industry with material.

Another source of popular culture was the lecture circuit. Controversial lecturers such as Theodore Weld, Lucy Stone, and Abby Kelley Foster abolitionized and were met with eggs and rocks. Paulina Wright Davis shocked female listeners by using a mannequin to illustrate her lectures on physiology and hygiene. Dio Lewis started the temperance Crusade with his lectures. Men and women signed on with various lecture companies, especially Lyceum and Chautauqua.

Education, some have said, was the religion of the age. Initially schooling was left to private initiative and benevolence. Some northern states had primary school systems, but though they were open to all, the fees required effectively banned most poor children. Horace Mann, who became head of the newly created Massachusetts Board of Education in 1837, campaigned for "common schools," open to all, free to all, with a common curriculum. He also encouraged the founding of "normal schools" to train teachers, mostly young women. Catharine Beecher, Lyman's oldest daughter, opened several such schools in Hartford, Connecticut, and Cincinnati, Ohio, to train missionary teachers for the West and South. After the war, women abolitionists like Sally Holley and Laura Haviland brought education to the emancipated slaves.

Primarily due to religious competition, colleges spread across the country. In 1880, England had only four degree-granting institutions of higher learning; Ohio alone had thirty-seven! The earliest high schools and colleges, such as Harvard and Yale, were for men only. Thus Emma Willard crusaded for her *Plan for Improving Female Education,* which led to the founding in 1821 of Troy Female Seminary. Mary Lyon opened Mount Holyoke in 1837. The first truly coeducational, biracial college was Oberlin Collegiate Institute, opened in 1833. Its graduates and influence led to the founding of a number of similar colleges across the Midwest: Knox, Wheaton, Berea. Public high school education developed in the latter half of the century. Education for children became compulsory. Education for adults became professionalized. Unlike Finney, who was taught by fellow minister George Gale, most ministers thereafter attended theological seminaries—at least in "respectable" denominations. Midwives were replaced by male medical school graduates. Lawyers no longer read law—as Henry Stanton did with Elizabeth's father, Judge Daniel Cady—but attended law schools. Professional and graduate schools were largely closed to women.

DIFFERENT SPHERES

At the center of this whirlwind of change was the American family. The Puritan family, the colonial family was tightly knit; multi-generational; the fulcrum of church, economy, and society. Families were the backbone of the social order. Parents, male and female, were in charge; children were miniature adults. Everyone had his or her own place and found security in it. Everyone worked together on the family farm or in the family business. Parents watched over not only their children but also grandparents, aunts and uncles, apprentices, slaves, indentured servants, and orphans. Women were strong,

competent, and courageous. All sat together at church in the
family pew; all met for family prayers. As late as 1820 in
Rochester, New York, everyone still lived and worked in the
same area of the city.

But by 1825 masters had moved to big houses in residential
neighborhoods, away from the business district. It signaled a
drastic change in the family. Society was becoming a divided
realm, "man's world" and "woman's sphere," public and
private. The world belonged now to men, the dirty realm of
business and politics, where power resided and the "important"
decisions were made. Ambition, competition, self-assertion,
and self-interest were its values. Personal morality no longer
coincided with business ethics. The home was the place for the
family, now reduced to absent father, cloistered mother, and
fewer and fewer children—the birthrate has steadily declined
since 1800. Mother was in charge but without real authority.
Workers lived unsupervised in boarding houses and tenements.
The slaves were freed, and only the Irish maid sometimes lived
in. Occasionally a grandparent came to stay, but maiden aunts
lived alone or with each other. "Work" took place in the
business district or in the factory; the home was the place for
"leisure." Altruism, self-sacrifice, and humility were appropriate values for women only. Children were carefree; adolescents
were troubled only by longer periods of education since their
labor was unneeded in factories already filled with immigrants.
Religion, no longer allied with the magistrates in the rule of
society, was also relegated to woman's sphere, the private
realm. Historians have labeled it the cult of domesticity.
Barbara Welter's "Cult of True Womanhood: 1820–1860"
shows how the cult decreed that women should be pure,
submissive, religious, and domestic.

Reported Alexis de Tocqueville after his visit to America in
1831, "in no country has such constant care been taken as in
America to trace two clearly distinct lines of action for the two
sexes." For women the result was a major crisis. In colonial
times everyone's work was essential to the domestic economy.
Now in the new age, career choices for men widened, and their
work took them farther and farther from the hearth. Low-paid
Irish servants and black maids took over the housework for the
middle class; schools took the children; and factory-produced

bread, clothing, soap, and candles took away the need for crafts and skills. The middle-class woman no longer had any work to do that society recognized as such. Women became luxuries, to be supported by men—fathers and husbands. Searching for meaning and usefulness, they plunged into revivals, religious reform, missions, social work, and creative pursuits. They began to protest the ideological cult of domesticity which sought to keep them in their place, to keep them pure, submissive, religiously orthodox, and domesticated. In short, feminist consciousness began to dawn.

CHAPTER 3

A CURE FOR "BETWEENITY"

You can and you can't;
You will and you won't;
You're damned if you do;
And you're damned if you don't.

*C*harles Grandison Finney (1792–1874) said that many people of his day were caught in the dilemma illustrated by this popular jingle—a state of "betweenity." He illustrated the dilemma in his sermon "Traditions of the Elders" with a story about a woman "who had been a long time under conviction" of sin and had often asked her minister what she must do to be saved. In each conversation with her and in each Sunday sermon, the minister declared that sinners must repent but then always added a reminder of their helplessness and dependence on God. Sinners must pray and "use the means," he said, yet "wait patiently for God to change" their hearts.

One Sunday morning the minister neglected to add "his accustomed inconsistency, and after pressing sinners to immediate repentance, sat down without the usual addition that they could not." The woman, who immediately repented and obtained salvation, met him at the door with, "Why did you not tell me of this before?" The baffled pastor replied, "Why I have declared it to you every Sabbath." "Yes," replied the woman, "but always until now, you told me before you sat down, that I could not repent."

Although accused of immediatism, Finney told women and men simply to "repent and believe." Religion, he said, is not something to wait for, but something to do.

Finney himself had been a promising young lawyer in 1821, beginning to take his place in the social order of Adams, New York, courting the local belles, playing cello at the Presbyterian

Church. Then revivalist Jedediah Burchard arrived and, said Finney in his *Memoirs,* "I made up my mind that I would settle the question of my soul's salvation at once." It was "the 10th of October, and a very pleasant day." Finney spent it in Bible reading and prayer in the woods. Late in the afternoon he found that "all sense of sin, all consciousness of present sin or guilt had departed." He had "quiet of . . . mind," and his "heart was all liquid." Charles Finney had been converted, and the world would not be the same.

Finney was born 29 August 1792 in Warren, Connecticut, and his family migrated to Oneida County, New York, in 1794. Later they moved to Hanover on the shores of Lake Ontario. Finney attended Hamilton Oneida Academy in Clinton, southwest of Utica, for two years, and then the Warren (Connecticut) Academy for four years. After teaching school, he returned to Jefferson County, New York, and began to study law.

Upon his conversion he renounced the study of law and began to read theology with the local Presbyterian pastor, George W. Gale, who, according to Finney, "was of the old school type; that is, . . . thoroughly Calvinistic." Finney was admitted to the St. Lawrence Presbytery on 25 June 1823 and was granted a preaching license in December. He was ordained 1 July 1824, even though the presbytery was already concerned about his colloquial preaching. When asked if he accepted the Westminster Confession, he tactfully affirmed that he did, to the best of his understanding of it. He later claimed that he had not read it before his examination, and when he did he was appalled. "Theological fiction" was his usual description of it.

Finney's first pastoral assignment began 17 March 1824 as a missionary to Jefferson County. His $192 support came from the Female Missionary Society of the Western District of New York, the first such organization financially independent of the male religious establishment. Formerly called the Female Missionary Society of Oneida County, it was founded in 1814 from the Whitestown Female Charitable Society, itself founded in 1806, by members of the First Presbyterian Church, Utica. One of its leading members was Sophia Clarke. In October 1824 Finney married another of its members, Lydia Andrews

(1794–1847). Due to the outbreak of revival, it was six months before they lived together.

THE BURNED-OVER DISTRICT

Upstate New York had already experienced a number of revivals. In fact the nation was well into the Second Great Awakening, usually dated from the spontaneous outbreak of revival fervor and ecstatic exercises during camp meetings at Gasper River in southern Kentucky the last week in July 1800 and at Cane Ridge in eastern Kentucky in August 1801. Like wildfire that revival spirit blazed in Kentucky and moved east to Virginia and the Carolinas, south into Tennessee and Georgia.

The Finney revivals in the 1820s and 1830s were the culmination. His work began in the small towns of Jefferson, Lawrence, and Oneida counties and spread into the cities of Rome and Utica where he held forth through the winter of 1825–26, at Oneida County's spiritual center, First Presbyterian Church, pastored by Samuel Aiken. When Finney asked Aiken about the church's spiritual state, Aiken told him that "one of his principal women had been so deeply exercised in her soul about the state of the church and of the ungodly of that city that she had prayed for two days and nights almost incessantly."

That woman may well have been Sophia Clarke, wife of lawyer Erastus Clarke. They lived next door to the parsonage. She had been converted in the revival of 1813 and was one of the founders of Utica's Female Charitable Society and of its Maternal Society. She was also active in the Female Missionary Society, Moral Reform Society, and the Western Educational Society.

Sophia Clarke was particularly concerned about the soul of her nephew, a student at Hamilton College, who had been ridiculing the revivals. On the ruse that the despised Finney was not to speak at the morning service, "Aunt C" maneuvered her nephew into attending. "When we came to the pew door," he said later, she "motioned me to go in and followed with several ladies and shut me in." When Finney rose to speak and the nephew attempted to escape, she bent forward in prayer and blocked his way. She also guilt-tripped him with the whisper, "You'll break my heart if you go." Finney preached on "One

Sinner Destroyeth Much Good," and the errant nephew later said, "He just held me up on his toasting fork before the audience." Theodore Dwight Weld (1803–95) was soundly converted and became the leader of Finney's Holy Band and of the abolitionist movement.

It was in Utica that Finney's female converts first began testifying to their faith publicly in "promiscuous assemblies." Finney was charged with the practice, but Weld later took credit for the innovation in a letter to Angelina and Sarah Grimké:

> The very week that I was converted to Christ in the city of Utica during a powerful revival of religion under brother Finney—and the first time I ever spoke in a religious meeting—I urged females both to pray and speak if they felt deeply enough to do it, and not to be restrained from it by the fact that they were *females*. I made these remarks at a meeting when not less than two hundred persons were present of both sexes, and *five* ministers of the gospel at least, and I think more. The result was that seven females, a number of them the most influential female christians in the city, confessed their sin in being restrained by their sex, and prayed publickly in succession at that very meeting.

From Utica, Finney moved on to Auburn's First Presbyterian Church. In the congregation during the summer of 1826 and again in his meetings during the spring of 1831 was young Caroline Maria Seymour (Severance) (1820–1914). Her widowed mother had brought the family there in 1824 to live near her uncle, a Presbyterian "of the most pronounced type." She remembered for a lifetime the "revival meetings of the Reverends Burchard and Finney" as "excitements which recurred as regularly and inevitably as spring and fall housecleanings of that time, and which were as disturbing to the peace and routine of many homes."

From there Finney moved on to Troy. "The next happening in Troy that seriously influenced my character," Elizabeth Cady (1815–1902) recalled in *Eighty Years and More,* "was the advent of the Rev. Charles G. Finney, a pulpit orator, who, as a terrifier of human souls, proved himself the equal of Savonarola." As "the result of six weeks of untiring effort," said Cady, Troy experienced one of those intense revival seasons that swept over the city and through the seminary [Emma Hart Willard's Troy Female Seminary] like an epidemic, attacking in its worst form the most susceptible. Owing to my gloomy Calvinistic training in the Old Scotch Presbyterian church, and my vivid imagination, I was one of the first victims.

NEW LEBANON

Criticism of Finney's "new measures" had been coming from both the Unitarians and Universalists of upstate New York and from more conservative New England revivalists such as Asahel Nettleton and Lyman Beecher. In July 1827 equal numbers of Finneyites and eastern pastors met in New Lebanon, New York. Many of Finney's innovations were actually practices he had lifted from the Methodists (one review said Methodists were charging that "it was not fair to hurry [converts] into Calvinistic churches, before they had time to discover their proper home"). He was charged with such "heresies" as holding protracted meetings (every afternoon and evening rather than just on Sundays), using the anxious meeting and anxious or mourners' bench to single out those seeking salvation, denouncing settled pastors who opposed such meetings, preaching in a pungent manner, using colloquial language in the pulpit, hastily admitting converts to the church, using the "prayer of faith" to claim salvation rather than urging people to wait for it, and allowing women to pray and testify in promiscuous assemblies.

Discussions lasted for nine days, and the two camps managed to reach compromises on every issue save one: women's praying and testifying. The Finneyites would not agree to stifle it, and the easterners could not abide it. The lines were drawn, and the women won. In the context of Finney's revivals, if we are to analyze the correspondence and articles by Finney's critics, it was not just the right to speak but the right to pray *for people by name*—more especially, for pastors by name—which upset the critics. In essence the women won the right to differ; the right to criticize; the right to bring pressure on their husbands, their fellow citizens, and their religious establishment.

Undaunted, Finney went back to holding revivals in Wilmington, Delaware; Philadelphia, and Lancaster, Pennsylvania. In 1830 he held meetings in New York City at the request of the Association of Gentlemen, led by Arthur and Lewis Tappan, who founded the First Free Presbyterian Church on revivalist principles. Pews were free to all, not just those able to pay.

From New York Finney returned upstate to Rochester from 10 September 1830 to 6 March 1831. Even Beecher eventually conceded that "this was the greatest work of God, and the greatest revival of religion, that the world has ever seen, in so short a time." It was in Rochester that Finney made reform a part of his message, speaking out on temperance. Membership in Rochester's churches doubled in six months.

The *Observer* noted that converts included "men of wealth, talents, and influence." One was deputy county clerk and editor of the *Monroe Telegraph*, Henry Brewster Stanton, who became a member of the Holy Band, an abolitionist with Theodore Weld, and husband to Elizabeth Cady. Another was a farmer from nearby Henrietta, Joseph Brown, along with several of his older children. Antoinette (1825–1921) was too young to attend, but her mother gathered the younger children around her knee to hear Scripture and to pray. Antoinette publicly confessed her faith 5 May 1834 and joined the Congregational church where Joseph had become a deacon. Paulina Kellogg (Wright Davis) (1813–76) was a teen-ager when Finney arrived in Rochester. An orphan living with a very strict and orthodox Presbyterian aunt, she had joined the church at thirteen but "suffered constant torment from her sins, and found comfort only in the religious enthusiasm of recurrent revivals." She dreamed of becoming a missionary but in 1833 married Francis Wright, a wealthy Presbyterian Utica merchant. Together they plunged into reform activities—moral reform, temperance, abolition, and woman's rights. She said it was discussions about whether or not women should be permitted to speak and pray in revivals that roused her on the woman question.

The Wrights were typical of Finney's converts. Previous reformers had wanted to control the excesses of their neighbors; the Finneyites wanted to liberate them from their sins. Through individual conversion and public example, eventually through mass politics and legislation, they attempted to eliminate sin from society and bring the millennium on earth.

From upstate New York, the revival moved west into Ohio and Michigan, east into the major seaboard cities. It precipitated a controversy which put an end to Presbygationalism, the cooperation of Presbyterians and Congregationalists on the frontier which had been worked out in the Plan of Union of 1801 and the Plan of Accommodation in 1808. It split the Presbyterians in 1837 into Old School Princetonians and New School revivalists.

From Rochester, Finney went to Boston and finally settled down in New York City in April 1832 to become pastor of the Second Free Presbyterian Church. Lewis Tappan had leased the Chatham Street Theater for his friend and outfitted it as a chapel seating two thousand people. Each May it became the meeting place for the annual conventions of the Benevolence Empire. It was there in 1835 that Finney gave his famous *Lectures on Revivals of Religion,* in which he articulated a theology and methodology of revivals still read by modern evangelicals. In 1836 he resigned from the Presbyterian Church and became a Congregationalist, pastoring New York's Sixth Free Church, better known as Broadway Tabernacle.

OBERLIN

Though Finney kept his New York pastorate, in the spring of 1835 the Finney family moved to Oberlin, Ohio. Finney's Holy Band had fled Lyman Beecher's Lane Seminary in Cincinnati because the trustees prohibited further discussions of immediate abolition. They came to Oberlin on the condition that Finney be their theology professor. The president was to be Lane trustee and Cincinnati Presbyterian pastor Asa Mahan (1799–1889). He too was a product of the burned-over district, reared by a mother who was "one of the greatest female thinkers and readers on religious topics" that he ever met. He too was a graduate of Hamilton, and of Andover Theological Seminary, licensed by the Oneida Presbytery. Mahan asked that his epitaph read: "The first man, in the history of the race, who conducted woman, in connection with members of the opposite sex, through a full course of liberal education."

"Men came to Oberlin for various reasons," said Lucy Stone, "women, because they had nowhere else to go." Lucy (1818–93) was enrolled there between 1843 and 1847. She had joined the West Brookfield, Massachusetts, Congregational Church as a child, but she was offended when a member was expelled for antislavery activities and her vote supporting him was ignored. Stone enrolled at Mount Holyoke but stayed only three months because Mary Lyon was upset at her leaving copies of William Lloyd Garrison's *Liberator* in the reading room and turning her missionary mite box into one for the American Anti-Slavery Society.

Lucy's friend at Oberlin and her future sister-in-law was Antoinette Brown. She came for two reasons: her older brother was a graduate of the theological department, and "our beloved Professor Finney" taught theology. She admitted, however, that

> there was considerable difference of opinion on the woman question among the faculty, still more among the students. President Mahan was one of the more liberal and Professor Finney thought that exceptional women might be called upon to become religious teachers.

Brown arrived in 1846, completed the ladies' course in one year and, without encouragement even from Stone, enrolled in the theological course. She completed it in 1850, though the school refused to grant her a degree or encourage her ordination.

Another classmate of Brown and Stone was Sallie Holley (1818–93). Born in Canandaigua, New York, Sallie was the daughter of a Methodist mother and an abolitionist father, Myron Holley. She came to Oberlin in 1847. Her 1851 graduation speech, entitled "Ideal of Womanhood," included the right of women to vote and preach. Hannah Conant Tracy (Cutler) (1815–96), born in Massachusetts and reared in Ohio, was determined to go to Oberlin, but her father forbade it. Instead in 1834 she married John Tracy, a theology student who became an abolitionist lecturer. She read theology and then law. When her husband died in 1844 as a result of a beating received while aiding a slave, Hannah wrote and taught until she had funds to enroll at Oberlin 1847–48. She participated with Stone and Brown in the debating society of women, which met in the woods and in the home of an elderly black woman because college officials still were not sure that rhetoric was a proper skill for women.

Another contemporary was Josephine Abiah Penfield (Cushman Bateham) (1829–1901). When she was four, her father died and her mother remarried the Reverend Henry Cowles, professor of Greek, Latin, and Old Testament literature at Oberlin. Josephine graduated in 1847 and married a graduate of the theological department. He died during their year of missionary service in Haiti. She then married Michael Bateham, founder and editor of the *Ohio Cultivator.* Like her mother, she had contributed to the *Oberlin Evangelist.* She edited the ladies' department for the *Cultivator* and opened its pages to discussions of woman's rights, education, peace, and temperance. From 1884 to 1896 she was superintendent of the WCTU's Department for the Suppression of Sabbath Desecration.

One of the earliest women graduates was Betsey Mix Cowles (1810–76). A Connecticut Yankee whose father took a Congregational pastorate in Ohio, Cowles enrolled in Oberlin in 1838 and completed the ladies' course in 1840. Henry Cowles was her kin.

Finney's own concept of woman's role expanded with his second marriage in 1848 to Elizabeth Ford Atkinson (d. 1863), a widow from Rochester. In November 1849 they made their first trip to England and found that Mrs. Finney was also welcome as a speaker. According to Finney's *Memoirs,* she "put the women of Scotland very much in a new position, in regard to personal efforts in revivals of religion." When they returned to Hartford, Connecticut, and Syracuse, New York, in 1853, "here again Mrs. Finney established her ladies' meetings with great success."

The Finneys spent the years 1858–60 in England. His health failing, in 1865 he resigned the presidency of Oberlin, which he had assumed from Mahan in 1850, but he continued as pastor of Oberlin's First Congregational Church until 1872. Also in

1865 he married Rebecca A. Rayl (d. 1907), assistant principal of Oberlin's ladies' department. Finney died at Oberlin 16 August 1875.

AN ARMINIANIZED THEOLOGY

Theologically as well as methodologically, Finney represented a shift. As Lucy Aiken wrote William Channing in 1828: "They have gradually and almost imperceptibly quitted Calvinism for Arminianism." While this certainly applies to the Unitarians of Boston, it also applies to the New School revivalists, Finney and friends—which may account in part for why so many Finneyites, especially women, felt just as comfortable in the Unitarian church as they grew older. Although the Presbygationalists considered Methodists more emotional and of a somewhat lower class, they gradually adopted a theology close to John Wesley's evangelical Arminianism.

One central issue was the doctrine of sin. Traditional Calvinism believed that humanity as a whole participated in original sin because Adam, as its federal head, transgressed God's command. Thus the *New England Primer* declared: "In Adam's fall/We sinned all." All suffer from innate depravity imparted at conception and cannot escape unless God, in inscrutable sovereignty, elects us to salvation. Unitarian Channing totally rejected the natural depravity of children, and Harvard professor Henry Ware declared them by nature innocent and pure.

The Finneyites would not go quite that far, but they did reject the federal concept of original sin and argued that free agency was inherent in human persons who possess understanding, conscience, and will. The world is such that people voluntarily commit sinful acts as soon as they become moral agents. They agreed with Yale theologian Nathaniel William Taylor, who declared that moral depravity is a person's "own act, consisting in a free choice of some object rather than God, as his chief good;—or a free preference of the world and of worldly good, to the will and glory of God." Said Finney, infants are "neither sinful or holy, until they are moral agents, and render themselves so by obedience or disobedience to the moral law."

Thus all sin is voluntary rather than inherited and imputed. This rejection of infant damnation was particularly appealing to women. Calvinist women suffered deep anguish whenever children died, not knowing whether they would go to heaven or hell. Methodist women, on the other hand, tended to say, as Phoebe Palmer consoled herself and others repeatedly, that the child had gone to heaven so that the mother's heart might be centered there too.

For Finney, sin was defined as selfishness and willful disobedience to God's moral law. This implies a concept of free will and free moral agency. Said Finney in his *Lectures on Revivals of Religion,* to say that human beings do not have a free will "slanders God . . . , charging him with infinite tyranny, in commanding men to do that which they have no power to do." If sinners are unable to respond, if they must be given the Holy Spirit to enable them to obey the gospel, then common justice would compel God to give that Spirit to all before God could justly require repentance. In other words, "when God commands us to do a thing, it is the highest possible evidence that we can do it . . . equivalent to an oath that we can do it. He has no right to command, unless we have power to obey." God has commanded us to repent; *ipso facto* we must have the ability to do so.

This belief in human agency freed middle and upper classes of responsibility for controlling and governing a sinful humankind and turned them toward converting sinners and trying to perfect the world. Sin, disorder, and social evil would disappear if everyone would choose good, make unselfish choices, and convince everyone else to do likewise.

Obviously Finney no longer believed in election and a limited atonement. Salvation was freely available to all. No need to wait to see if one were among the elect. Since sin was a voluntary act and free agency was not destroyed by the Fall, salvation was available to anyone who would voluntarily turn from selfishness, ask God's forgiveness, and in faith claim salvation (i.e., pray the "prayer of faith"). Said Finney derisively, "Religion is something to *do,* not something to *wait for.*"

Finney's theology, very similar to the New Haven theology or the New Divinity being expounded at Yale University, was an attempt to modify Calvinism to fit a revivalist methodology. Some have argued that revivalism was essentially an American propaganda technique necessary in a society where religion had been disestablished and religious options were numerous. However, central to this Arminianized theology was a belief in the moral government of God. God is the moral governor of the world. All persons have the intelligence and freedom to choose—they are free moral agents. Thus they are under moral obligation. The highest good is the glory of God, the well-being of the moral governor. Choice of this ensures an individual's own best interests and the happiness of the universe. The correlation of such a theology with reform is obvious.

CHAPTER 4

"BE YE HOLY!"

HOLINESS is POWER!
—*Phoebe Palmer*

*D*uring a revival meeting for "prayer, praise, and inquiry" at Oberlin during October 1836, a recent graduate arose to ask President Mahan and Professor Finney: "When we look to Christ for sanctification, what degree of sanctification may we expect from him? May we look to him to be sanctified wholly, or not?"

Knowing that it was a very delicate question, President Mahan replied that they would have to give the question "prayerful and careful attention" and "in due time" they would give the student body a "full and specific answer."

Various forms of perfectionism, the belief that human beings can attain some form of perfection in this life, flourished in America in the 1830s and 1840s. It was an inherent part of the idealism which inspired national optimism and that sense of messianic destiny. Both the Mormons and the Shakers had perfectionist tendencies. A stronger movement, centered in Albany, New York, spread out east and west along the Erie Canal.

Most famous, or infamous, were the "antinomian perfectionists," who congregated around John Humphrey Noyes (1811–86), first in Putney, Vermont, and finally in Oneida, New York. Noyes experienced conversion in a Finney revival in 1831 and felt called to the ministry, spending a year at Andover and two years at Yale. When he began preaching perfectionism, his Congregational preaching license was revoked, and when he elaborated his ideas in the *Perfectionist,* a journal he published 1834–36, he was denied ordination. Noyes remains famous because his community at Oneida after 1848 practiced a form of sexual sharing called complex marriage, and economic sharing called Bible communism. In 1880 the community became a corporation which still manufactures silver flatware.

Noyes taught that it was scriptural for Christians to expect to be able to live totally sinless lives. He argued that this was the logical outcome of New Haven Calvinist theology. If one believed in election by grace and the perseverance of the saints, then perfection should be a natural result. If sin lies wholly in the will and persons have the ability to obey the moral law, then in Christ people should be able to attain perfection. To profess holiness is only to acknowledge God's gift, said Noyes. In order to be holy, one simply has to claim it. If one is perfect, then all one does is holy. True Christians cannot sin, declared Noyes. Others called it antinomian.

News of Noyes's ideas quickly reached Oberlin. In fact, articles from the *Perfectionist* had been reprinted in Cincinnati newspapers and debated at Lane Seminary before the Finneyite students left there. Two questions concerned perfectionists in general: (1) whether or not total sinlessness is possible—a doctrinal, theological question; and (2) whether or not "perfect" Christians are bound by conventional ethical constraints—a practical, ethical question. Noyes obviously concerned himself and his community with the second. Mahan and Finney were much more concerned with the first.

They spent the winter of 1836–37 in New York City, pondering the question, struggling with such Scriptures as "the very God of peace sanctify you wholly; and I pray God your whole spirit and soul and body be preserved blameless unto the coming of our Lord Jesus Christ" (I Thess. 5:23) and "Be ye therefore perfect, even as your Father which is in heaven is perfect" (Matt. 5:48). They both read John Wesley's *Plain Account of Christian Perfection.* They may well have been exposed to the classics holiness women most often read: the lives of Hester Ann Rogers and Mary Bosanquet Fletcher, wife of Wesley's most eloquent champion of the doctrine, John Fletcher.

THE SECOND BLESSING

Although John Wesley taught a concept of holiness, entire sanctification, or, as he preferred to call it, perfect love, the American Methodist church had to some extent neglected the idea in its quest to become the nation's leading denomination and representative church. The idea was being revived and reworked, however, by two sisters in New York City: Sarah Worrall Lankford (Palmer) (1806–96) and Phoebe Worrall Palmer (1807–74). Both had experienced conversion at early ages and joined the Methodist church. Sarah married a merchant, and Phoebe married Walter C. Palmer, trained as a physician at the New York City College of Physicians and Surgeons, a practitioner of homeopathic medicine. (Sarah Lankford married Walter Palmer after Phoebe Palmer's death.)

On 21 May 1835 at 2:30 P.M., Sarah Lankford affirmed that she experienced the assurance of entire sanctification. In August she consolidated prayer meetings at the Allen Street and Mulberry Street Methodist churches into one meeting at the home the Lankfords shared with the Palmers. Known around the world as the Tuesday Meeting for the Promotion of Holiness, it endured for more than sixty years and spawned similar meetings everywhere.

Although Phoebe was a member of the group, she herself did not experience holiness until "the evening of July 26th, 1837, between the hours of eight and nine o'clock" when

> the Lord gave me such a view of my utter pollution and helplessness, apart from the cleansing, energizing influences of the purifying blood of Jesus, and the quickening aids of the Holy Spirit, that I have ever since retained a vivid realization of the fact.

She was to become the more famous of the sisters, leading holiness revivals and camp meetings in this country, Canada, and the British Isles. Through her books, she substantially changed the concept.

Though Finney and Mahan undoubtedly were influenced by Palmer and the Methodist conception of holiness, the Tuesday Meeting was for women only until December 1839 when

Phoebe L. Upham visited and wished to bring along her husband, Congregational theologian Thomas Upham, professor at Bowdoin College in Maine. From then on the meetings were open to anyone and drew regular participation from around the world, including bishops, clergy, college and seminary faculty members as well as laypersons from a variety of denominations. Yet usually Sarah or Phoebe presided, and every person present, male or female, was free to give a testimony or to pray.

During the winter of 1836–37, in which Finney and Mahan explored the issue of holiness, Mahan felt that he experienced a second work of grace in which Christ "filled and occupied the entire compass of his being." Finney did not enter into the same experience until 1843, but he began preaching their conclusions about Christian perfection almost immediately. Two sermons on the topic were given at Broadway Tabernacle and reprinted in his *Letters to Professing Christians.* He noted in his *Memoirs* that, "in looking at the state of the Christian church, as it had been revealed to me in my revival labors," he was led "earnestly to inquire whether there was not something higher and more enduring than the Christian church was aware of; whether there were not promises, and means provided in the Gospel for the establishment of Christians in altogether a higher form of Christian life."

OBERLIN PERFECTIONISM

Upon their return to Oberlin, Finney and Mahan began to explain the doctrine to their students. As word spread, controversy raged. To explain their views in contradistinction to rumors which linked them with Noyes, the faculty began the *Oberlin Evangelist.* The first issue, 1 November 1838, contained a sermon by Mahan entitled "Is Perfection in Holiness Attainable in This Life?" which became a chapter in *The Scripture Doctrine of Christian Perfection,* published in 1839. His answer to the question was affirmative.

Opponents, particularly Old School Calvinists (Princeton's Benjamin Warfield wrote *Perfectionism* as a critique of the movement) charged that Oberlin Perfectionism, as it came to be called (Oberlin people preferred to speak of the "doctrine of

Christian Perfection"), was simply a logical extension of Nathaniel Taylor's New Divinity. With Taylor, Finney and Mahan distinguished between a sinful, depraved nature (i.e., all human beings do inevitably sin) and depravity of the will (human beings do have free, undepraved wills and thus they do not sin by necessity). Thus people can will to be perfect, just as they can will to be converted. People are morally depraved because they freely will things that are contrary to the will of God. Perfection to the Finneyites was not perfect living (à la Noyes), but right willing (for Wesley it had been perfect loving). It was not like God's perfection (omnipotence, eternity, immutability) or perfect knowledge or freedom from temptation or sinless ethical and moral behavior. Rather it was "perfect obedience to the law of God." Since the will is free of any innate limitations on moral ability, persons can receive instantaneous power from Christ to will correctly. The New Haven Calvinists agreed that morality was based on free will, and therefore perfection a logical possibility, but they refused to admit that anyone actually achieved it. Finney lashed out at this equivocation in the same way he had at their hesitation to use means to claim salvation.

The Oberlin theologians clearly drew on Methodist sources as well. When Mahan's book appeared, George Peck, editor of the *Methodist Quarterly Review* and author of his own book, *Christian Perfection,* concluded that "though it is not to be maintained that he expresses himself Methodistically upon all the points of this great doctrine, we are satisfied that the thing which we mean by Christian Perfection is truly set forth in that work." Warfield agreed and called the first half dozen years of Oberlin Perfectionism its Wesleyan period. Mahan was particularly careful to declare sanctification, like salvation, a gift of God's grace and not something to be attained solely by human effort. Finney tended toward more emphasis on human ability. In 1859 Mahan became president of the Wesleyan Methodists' Adrian (Michigan) College.

ON THE ALTAR

Phoebe Palmer was reshaping the concept at the same time in her books *The Way of Holiness* (1843), *Faith and Its Effects*

(1849), and *Present to My Christian Friend on Entire Devotion to God* (1853). She said that she was encouraged to do so by a question from a Presbyterian minister, "whether there is not a *shorter way.*" She carefully declared repeatedly that "not Wesley, not Fletcher, not Finney, not Mahan, not Upham, but the Bible" was the source of her formulation. In adapting holiness to American revivalism, she made it a second blessing, quite similar in structure to Finney's description of conversion. Finney saw conversion as the beginning of the Christian life rather than something of a culmination to be awaited. Wesley had seen entire sanctification, or perfect love, as the culmination of the Christian's life, possibly attained shortly before death although he himself never claimed to attain it. Palmer saw sanctification as a second crisis experience inaugurating a life of holiness.

Considerable controversy was generated by the language Palmer began to use in the late 1840s. She argued that it came straight from Scripture, but Methodists called it un-Wesleyan and non-Methodists called it confusing. Palmer described the first step as "laying one's all on the altar." From Exodus 29:37, Matthew 23:19, and Romans 12:1-2, she deduced that Christ was the altar and that the altar sanctified the gift. Thus once one determined

> to consecrate all upon the altar of sacrifice to God, with the resolve to "enter into the bonds of an everlasting covenant to be wholly the Lord's for time and eternity," and then acting in conformity with this decision, *actually laying all upon the altar*

then, "by the most unequivocal Scripture testimony," they were obliged to *"believe that the sacrifice became the Lord's property; and by virtue of the altar upon which the offering was laid, became 'holy' and 'acceptable.' "* Wesley had emphasized that one was assured of sanctification by the witness of the Spirit. Like Finney, Palmer argued that one did not need to wait. If one met the conditions, then one could simply claim the promised blessing, though she did testify to having the witness of the Spirit.

Palmer, like Finney, emphasized the individual will. According to another woman evangelist, Palmer "would say so often, 'God *wills* that you should be holy. This is the will of God, even your sanctification; is it your will?' She was an Arminian to the core. 'Your *choice*—what is it?' " And she stressed human ability to activate the will: "Is God unreasonable in his requirements? Hath he given the command 'Be ye holy,' and not given the ability, with the command, for the performance of it?" During the Palmers' visit to the Old World from 1860 to 1864, an elderly man told her he was "waiting these thirty years for a special call." She asked if he believed the Bible and he said yes. To which she replied:

> Now, act on the principle that you really do believe what you profess to believe; that is, that the Bible is the word of God to you, because he has been saying to you ever since your childhood, "Son, give me thy heart." Resolve you will do it NOW. It is not knowledge you need, but ACTION.

THE MILLENNIUM

Perfectionism was not understood as merely a personal experience (though the later holiness movement came to stress only that aspect). It was also a social philosophy. As Palmer's biographer explains, "Entire sanctification, as a moral condition, involves, and that necessarily, an inherent operative energy, to be divinely guided in seeking to glorify God, and to meliorate society in the mass, and also as to the individuals which compose it."

Like many revivalists before and since, Charles Finney believed that the conversion of individuals would create a better society. He continually stressed the necessity for committed Christians to involve themselves in the reforms of the day. Imbibing the mood of optimism, he and others assumed that their efforts in revival and reform would usher in the millennium, the thousand-year reign of the kingdom of God on earth. For example, Lyman Beecher once declared his task to be "the promotion of revivals of religion . . . as a prominent instrumentality for the conversion of the world, and the speedy introduction of the millennial reign of our Lord Jesus Christ."

Revivals were the beginning, perfection the second step. In

the initial issue of the *Oberlin Evangelist,* the editors declared that one reason for its publication was "to call attention of Christians to the fact the Millennium is to consist in the entire sanctification of the church." Another journal, *Beauty of Holiness,* saw a similar vision: "Are not these meetings for holiness . . . the germs, the dawnings of millennial glory? Are they not strikingly imitative of the pentecostal? . . . Is not this the baptism now called for, . . . ere the world blossoms as a rose?" They were further encouraged when a revival, begun among New York businessmen, spread holiness teaching coast to coast via telegraph lines in 1857 and 1858.

Similarly women saw the increase of attention to woman's rights as a sign of the approaching millennium. The call for the first National Woman's Rights Convention in Worcester, Massachusetts, in 1850, contained this declaration as its second paragraph:

> The upward-tending spirit of the age, busy in a hundred forms of effort for the world's redemption from the sins and sufferings which oppress it, has brought this one, which yields to none in importance and urgency, into distinguished prominence. One half of the race are its immediate objects, and the other half are as deeply involved, by that absolute unity of interest and destiny which nature has established between them.

The call goes on to state:

> By the inspiration of the Almighty, the beneficent spirit of reform is roused to the redress of these wrongs. . . . It is the spirit of reviving truth and righteousness which has moved upon the great deep of the public heart, and roused its redressing justice; and through it, the Providence of God is vindicating the order and appointments of his creation.

Angelina Grimké, in a letter to her friend Jane Smith dated 10 August 1837, declared, "I am persuaded that woman is not to be as she has been, a mere secondhand agent in the regeneration of a fallen world, but the acknowledged equal and coworker with man in this glorious work."

CHAPTER 5

RELIGION IS SOMETHING TO DO

It is not a question of feeling *but of* willing *and* action.

—*Charles Grandison Finney*

*E*lizabeth Cady Stanton was a teen-ager, a student at Emma Willard's Troy Female Seminary, when "one of those intense revival seasons . . . swept over the city and thus the seminary like an epidemic, attacking in its worst form the most susceptible." Stanton, as she admits in *Eighty Years and More,* was "one of the first victims."

She soon found herself on the anxious seat, a pew reserved for those concerned about their soul's salvation. "There," she said, "we learned the total depravity of human nature and the sinner's awful danger of everlasting punishment." Fortunately,

> in the depths of your despair you were told that it required no herculean effort on your part to be transformed into an angel, to be reconciled to God. . . . The way to salvation was short and simple. We had naught to do but to repent and believe and give our hearts to Jesus, who was ever ready to receive them.

How to do that was the question, so she asked Dr. Finney: "I cannot understand what I am to do. If you should tell me to go to the top of the church steeple and jump off, I would readily do it, if thereby I could save my soul; but I do not know how to go to Jesus."

"Repent and believe," was Finney's simple reply. "That is all you have to do to be happy here and hereafter."

Stanton was not the only person who took his advice. Her future husband, Henry Stanton, was converted in Rochester.

Antoinette Brown's father and older siblings experienced salvation under the ministry of Finney; she was converted within the family circle and joined the Congregational church on profession of faith. Paulina Wright Davis "found comfort" in revivals. Mary Rice Livermore experienced conversion as a Baptist but was never sure she was among the elect. Both Angelina (1805–79) and Sarah Grimké (1792–1873) were "deeply stirred by a revival meeting" in their native Charleston, South Carolina, under Presbyterian auspices, though their family was Episcopalian. Phoebe Palmer and her sister Sarah Lankford were converted among the Methodists. Lucy Stone, Hannah Cutler, Josephine Bateham, and Betsey Cowles were members of revivalist churches where testimony to conversion was a membership requirement.

FREE MORAL AGENTS

A conversion experience had been a requirement for church membership among the Puritans—adults must "own the covenant" for themselves. Believing that such an experience was a sign of God's election, they prayed, listened intently to instruction, and waited for something to happen to them. When it did not happen to second-generation Puritans in Massachusetts Bay Colony, ministers adopted the "Half-Way Covenant": baptized believers could have their children baptized, but they still could not take communion and participate as full members themselves. Jonathan Edwards repudiated this compromise and insisted on conversion. For many it came in the First Great Awakening.

Finney too insisted on the necessity of conversion, but he presented it in a different way. Antoinette Brown said that her father "had accepted the Calvinistic idea that it was God who must convert him in his own time and had waited years for that time to come." Then he went to Finney's meetings and learned that "Prof. Finney laid the whole stress of his preaching on the duty of the sinner himself to work actively for his own conversion. Although a partial Calvinist, he had in that matter taken a new departure."

Finney gave conversion a structure, a formula. At the heart of his theology was a belief in free will. God commands sinners

to repent, and thus they must have the power to do so. "When
God commands us to do a thing, it is the highest possible
evidence that we can do it," said Finney. "God has no right to
command, unless we have power to obey." Thus, "conversion
consists in the right employment of the sinner's own agency."
When people are confronted with their sin and the offer of
salvation, a decision is demanded—an act of the will. They must
examine their hearts. Said Finney, "God has put these states of
mind just as absolutely under your control as the motions of
your limbs." Some said that they could not repent, that they
must wait to "feel the Spirit." Said Finney, "It is often difficult
to make them see that all their 'cannot' consists in their
unwillingness and not in their inability. . . . We, as moral
agents, have the power to obey God, and are perfectly bound to
obey, and the reason we do not is, that we are unwilling. The
influences of the Spirit are wholly a matter of grace." Sinners
"ought to be made to see what God requires of them is to *will*
right. If they obey and submit with the *will,* the feelings will
adjust themselves in due time. It is not a question of *feeling* but
of *willing* and *acting."* Once one has made the right decision,
one must "pray the prayer of faith," testify to one's conversion,
join the church, and get to work converting one's family and
neighbors and reforming the world.

Once one was converted, one must testify to one's faith, said
Finney, "by *precept* and *example,* on every proper occasion, by
their lips, but mainly by their lives." Christians "should rebuke,
exhort, and entreat with all longsuffering and doctrine."
Phoebe Upham pointed her finger directly at the "puritan and
Presbyterian Churches" in a *Guide to Holiness* article in 1863
entitled "Woman's Freedom in Worship": "To *impart* what
one receives from God, is the out-going life of the new
Christ-nature. . . . How opposed then to the new Christ-
nature, and to God's Word, is the sealing of woman's lips in the
public exercises of the Church." In her diary entry for
26 February 1873, Phoebe Palmer mentioned receiving a letter
from a Presbyterian woman asking why women were seldom
allowed to testify in her congregation. Palmer mused,

> Is it not passing strange that persons of intelligence should allow
> themselves to be thus bound, when they know it is contrary to

the conscious urgings of the Spirit, and above all, to the direct and implied teaching of the WORD?

The Almighty says "to all who are made recipients of the free, boundless grace of God, . . . 'Ye are my witnesses,' '*You* know what I have done for *you*, therefore testify for *Me.*' "

Revivalists and holiness advocates, indeed, founded journals to give outlet to such testimonies. The first issue of the *Guide to Christian Perfection* contained a special notice on the last page:

A WORD to the Female Members of the CHURCH.—Many of you have experienced the grace of sanctification. Should you not then, as a thank-offering to God, give an account of this gracious dealing with your souls, that others may be partakers of this grace also? *Sisters in Christ,* may we not expect that you will assist us both with your prayers and pens?

A SHORTER WAY

Holiness or sanctification was attained by a similar process. John Wesley had taught that one made a commitment to the process of sanctification, but that attainment of perfect love was possible, if at all, shortly before death.

Phoebe Palmer declared that she wrote *The Way of Holiness* in response to a Presbyterian minister who asked her "whether there is not a *shorter way.*" After consideration, Palmer answered that indeed there was. God requires present holiness—did not God command, "Be ye holy" (Matt. 5:48)? The fact that God commanded it guarantees that it is possible. How? One must simply "consecrate all upon the altar of sacrifice to God," and then simply *"believe that the sacrifice became the Lord's property; and by virtue of the altar upon which the offering was laid, became 'holy' and 'acceptable.'"* Christ is the altar, and the altar sanctifies the gift. Again one need not wait for feeling. Said Palmer, simply "resolve that you WILL HAVE IT NOW, and it may be yours at once." And then testify to it. If one does not, one loses the experience.

An 1888 volume entitled *Forty Witnesses* gives the testimonies of such people as Mahan and Moody, Palmer and Lankford, Whitall Smith and Willard. They give evidence of this pattern. For example, Willard, converted in 1859, experienced holiness in 1866 under the ministry of "Dr. and Mrs. Phoebe Palmer." Her heart had been prepared by her reading of the *Life of Hester Ann Rogers, Life of Carvosso, Life of Mrs. Fletcher,* Wesley's *Sermons on Christian Perfection,* and copies of the *Guide to Holiness,* of which Palmer was now editor. After hearing Mrs. Palmer speak "with marvelous clearness and power," Willard, accompanied by her mother, went to the altar. "Kneeling in utter self-abandonment," she "consecrated [herself] anew to God." In her heart she categorized her "chief besetments" as "a speculative mind, a hasty temper, a too ready tongue, and a purpose to be a celebrated person," but "in that hour of sincere self-examination" she was humiliated to find that only the simple bits of jewelry she wore came up as "the separating causes" between herself and her Savior. When she "unconditionally yielded" her "petty little jewels," a "great peace" welled up in her soul and joy gradually possessed her. Unfortunately she kept quiet about her experience because her employers at the Genesee Wesleyan Seminary told her that "the Free Methodists have done great harm in Western New York by their excesses in the doctrine and experience of holiness." Willard, "young and docile-minded," kept still until she found that she had nothing in particular to speak about.

Most other women and men found the experience much more demanding. They felt God ask that their children, their spouses, sometimes their own reputations be laid on the altar. Finney, using Palmer's language in his *Memoirs,* tells of his struggles to lay his wife Lydia on the altar, perhaps because she was already in ill health. On top of that, many women felt compelled to let go of their resistance to public speaking. Whether or not God asked that initially, it was clear that all must testify to the experience to retain it. So speak out they must.

A DEMOCRATIC TENDENCY

This emphasis on the experience of conversion and sanctification had several ramifications. Initially it was very democratic. Traditional Puritan theology with its predestined elect encouraged a stratified society. Its view of conversion demanded passivity. It emphasized right doctrine, whose nuances could only be fully understood and appreciated by the ministerial elite.

Revivalism stressed experience and encouraged activity. All are sinners in need of salvation and sanctification. All are welcome and able to repent and believe, to consecrate themselves to holiness. Lyman Beecher was appalled when he heard that in Finney's revivals, "all men, because sinners, are therefore to be treated alike by ministers of the gospel without respect to age or station in society." He feared that this would result in a "leveling of all distinctions of society," which indeed it did. Women grasped the point immediately.

The key is that all persons are free moral agents. As Sarah Grimké notes in the first of her *Letters on the Equality of the Sexes:*

> God created us equal;—he created us free agents;—he is our Lawgiver, our King and our Judge, and to him alone is woman bound to be in subjection, and to him alone is she accountable for the use of those talents with which her Heavenly Father has entrusted her.

Angelina, in her *Letters to Catherine [sic] E. Beecher,* put it this way:

> Human beings have *rights,* because they are *moral* beings; . . . the mere circumstance of sex does not give to man higher rights and responsibilities, than to woman. . . . whatever it is morally right for man to do, it is morally right for woman to do.

Antoinette Brown went one step further in an address to the 1853 National Woman's Rights Convention in Cleveland: "That which is right, is right eternally, both for men and for women. Where God has given ability to act in any direction, he has given the right to act." Or as the women of the Boston Female Anti-Slavery Society said in 1835: "we cannot . . . believe that this garment of womanhood wherewith our souls are invested, debars us from the privileges or absolves us from the duties of a spiritual existence."

THE POWER TO SPEAK AND ACT

"Dear Darling, get the blessing of holiness, and it will be a gift of power," Sarah Lankford advised. Palmer declared that "holiness is a gift of power, and, when understandingly received by either old or young disciples, nerves for holy achievement." The experience transformed women particularly. Palmer's biographer, Richard Wheatley, recounts one example:

> In Tully [New York] Mrs. Palmer's loving instructions were blest, to the entire sanctification of a minister's wife, who was changed from a timid, shrinking, silent Christian, into one of tearful, modest, but pentecostal power, and who afterwards spoke in public, with remarkable effect.

Catherine Mumford Booth (1829–90), cofounder of the Salvation Army, was similarly transformed. In defense of Palmer's ministry in England in 1859, she had written *Female Ministry* during her pregnancy with Emma. During her confinement after the birth, God applied her arguments to her own heart. Three months later she confessed to her husband William's Methodist congregation that while they thought her a devoted, properly demure, and timid pastor's wife, she had been sinning against God. That night William asked her to preach, and she took as her text, "be filled with the Spirit." After that she "was never allowed to have another quiet Sabbath, when [she] was well enough to stand and speak."

Such behavior should not have surprised Finney because it was certainly in keeping with his warning that "you will be called eccentric, and probably you will deserve it." Said Finney,

> I never knew a person who was filled with the Spirit, that was not called eccentric. . . . they are unlike other people. . . . They act under different influences, take different views, are moved by different motives, led by a different spirit.

One cannot imagine a broader permission for socially deviant behavior.

THE POWER TO CHALLENGE

Participation in revivalism and in the conversion experience led to a questioning of traditional ways of thinking. Matilda

Joslyn Gage (1826–98), a Baptist from Cicero, New York, long remembered "sitting up until midnight listening to the discussions" carried on by her parents and "a large number of clergymen, who yearly held 'protracted meetings' in the place," concerning "baptism, original sin, predestination, and other doctrinal points." Paulina Wright Davis "was roused to thought on woman's position by a discussion in the church as to whether women should be permitted to speak and pray in promiscuous assemblies." Certain deacons in her church had "protested against a practice, in ordinary times, that might be tolerated during seasons of revival." But "those who had discovered their gifts in times of excitement were not so easily remanded to silence; and thus the Church was distracted then as now with the troublesome question of woman's rights."

Such experiences were intended to be empowering. In an 1864 series of editorials on "Model Revival" in the *Guide to Holiness,* Palmer declared:

> There is ever one standing in their midst, who baptizeth with the Holy Ghost and with fire. The gift is truly for the Marys and the Susannas as for the Peters and Johns. When the Holy Ghost descended, it fell alike upon them all. . . . There was a great work to be done, and therefore they *all* . . . spoke as the Spirit gave utterance.
>
> And who would dare to say that Christianity has lost any of its power. Spirit-beings men and women are still mighty in their sayings and doings.

Just as Finney had the audacity to question George Gale's theology when it did not correspond to Finney's experience, so Antoinette Brown rejected the authority of others:

> Mrs. [Lydia] Finney, having heard that I intended to study theology appealed to me not to do so, at least not to become a public speaker or minister. When she had brought many stereotyped arguments her last appeal was, "You will never feel yourself wise enough to go directly against the opinions of all the great men of the past." As that was exactly what her husband had done and was doing, it was necessary for me to reply, "That is exactly what Professor Finney is doing, and we all feel that he is making a great advance of thought."

Thus Brown studied theology against the advice of her family, most of the Oberlin faculty, and even her friend Lucy Stone. Repeatedly at the early woman's rights conventions she stood, Bible in hand, and met the challenges offered by the movement's clerical critics.

THE POWER TO OVERCOME PREJUDICE

The experience of conversion and sanctification unleashed a power within Christian society which potentially eradicated racial and sexual prejudices, a necessary step for those who were to advocate significant social change.

Finney's personal record is not entirely unblemished. Though his opponents called him an amalgamationist in matters of race, he was not. He welcomed blacks into his churches and at Oberlin, but he still seems to have favored social separation. His followers went much further. What really disturbed the citizens of Cincinnati about his Holy Band of abolitionist students at Lane was that they practiced what they preached. They mixed socially with black families and started schools and other social services for free blacks in the city. Weld lived with a black family. The Finneyite abolitionists were often the more radical in their social views, able to view blacks more nearly as equals. When the Grimké sisters learned that two black young men were in reality their nephews, they made them welcome in their home and paid for their education.

The power of Christian experience to overcome prejudices also worked from blacks toward whites. Holiness evangelist Amanda Berry Smith (1837–1915) reported that on the same day she was sanctified, her fear of whites was removed: "Somehow," she said, "I always had a fear of white people—that is, I was not afraid of them in the sense of doing me harm, or anything of that kind—but a kind of fear because they were white, and were there, and I was black and here!" Reminded by God of Galatians 3:28 ("There is neither Jew nor Greek, there is neither bond nor free, there is neither male nor female: for ye are all one in Christ Jesus"), she understood: "But now the Holy Ghost had made it clear to me. And as I looked at white people that I had always seemed to be afraid of, now they looked so small. The great mountain had become a mole-hill."

In her public ministry in this country and around the world, she found, however, that "some people don't get enough of the blessing to take prejudice out of them, even after they are sanctified." Some were prejudiced on account of her race; others on account of her sex. Usually, though, their prejudices vanished, and they found the blessing. Palmer testified to similar results. Rejoicing in her reception by ministers of Newark, New Jersey, she said:

What a mighty change has a practical reception of the doctrine produced. But a short time since, and the most of them would have condemned as fanatical, and perhaps as almost heretical, a female that would dare give in a testimony for God, before the Church. Now they invite and urge such testimonies.

CHAPTER 6

DIRECTLY TO THE BIBLE

The Bible is a wonderfully simple book.
—Phoebe Palmer

 *M*any women and men of the nineteenth century were far more steeped in the Bible than even scholars are today. Mary Rice Livermore (1820–1905), for example, noted in her autobiography, *The Story of My Life,* that prayer and Bible reading opened and closed each day in the Rice home. In addition, every child in the family from the age of seven was expected to read the Bible through once a year, according to a plan devised by her Baptist father. She observed the custom until she was twenty-three. Obviously, Scripture was totally ingrained in her memory. Her family called her the Family Concordance. When the death of her fifteen-year-old sister heightened her anxiety over the doctrine of election, she determined to read the Bible in the original, so she obtained a tutor and studied the Greek New Testament.

Elizabeth Cady was tutored in Greek by the Presbyterian pastor who lived next door. She began around age eleven when her only brother died, and her father sighed, "Oh, my daughter, I wish you were a boy!" Promising to try to take her brother's place, she thought that "the chief thing to be done in order to equal boys was to be learned and courageous." So she "decided to study Greek and learn to manage a horse." Thus she begged the pastor to teach her Greek. She also studied Latin and Greek with a class of boys at the local Johnstown Academy, receiving as a prize a Greek New Testament. When her pastor died, his will read: "My Greek lexicon, Testament, and grammar, and four volumes of Scott's commentaries, I will to Elizabeth Cady." She had them when she wrote *Eighty Years and More.* She was still wrestling with Scripture in 1895 and 1898 when she published *The Woman's Bible,* a two-volume collection of comments on various biblical passages.

One day when Lucy Stone was a child, she discovered Genesis 3:16, which declares that a woman's desire shall be for her husband and he will rule over her. "She knew that the laws and customs were against the women," notes her daughter and biographer Alice Stone Blackwell (1857–1950), "but it had never occurred to her that God could be against them." So she went to her mother and asked very seriously if there were anything she could take to make her die. When her mother found out why her child was contemplating suicide, she "consoled" her by pointing out other Scriptures which appear to have similar messages and told her that women are supposed to submit. "My mother always tried to submit. I never could," Stone later commented. Instead she vowed to go to college, study Greek and Hebrew until she could read the original text, and thus see for herself if in translation "men had falsified the text."

IN THE FINNEY TRADITION

Those in the revival tradition monitored their experience by Scripture and Scripture by their experience. Reason and common sense provided all the help they felt they needed to reach conclusions just as theologically valid as those of the eminent divines of their own and previous ages.

Even before his conversion, Charles Finney was comparing his own readings of the Bible with the preaching of George Gale and finding the pastor wrong. In his *Memoirs* he reports that soon after his conversion experience, he called on Gale to discuss the nature of the atonement, which Gale believed was limited to the elect. Finney "objected that this was absurd."

> I was however but a child in theology. I was but a novice in religion and in Biblical learning; but I thought he did not sustain his views from the Bible, and told him so. I had read nothing on

the subject except my Bible; and what I had there found upon
the subject, I had interpreted as I would have understood the
same and like passages in a law book.

Thus Finney outlined his hermeneutic. He did not interpret
Scripture from the standpoint of a predetermind system of
theology or treat it as some other-worldly mystery, but used his
own common sense. He considered the Bible inspired and
authoritative, yet a book to be flexibly applied to fit present
circumstances. As one of his former students wrote in the
Oberlin Quarterly Review (October 1849): "The Bible is
eminently a reasonable book."

Scripture, for Finney, was a source (not a measure) of
wisdom to those who took time to apply their mind to it. He
drew from it constantly in his own training for and practice of
ministry. He reports:

> Often when I left Mr. Gale, I would go to my room and spend a
> long time on my knees over my Bible. Indeed I read my Bible on
> my knees a great deal during those days of conflict, beseeching
> the Lord to teach me his own mind on those points. I had
> nowhere to go but directly to the Bible, and to the philosophy or
> workings of my own mind.

Finney believed that anyone could go directly to the Bible.
"Plain common sense" would lead them to understand and to
"believe that they mean just as they say." In his *Lectures on
Revivals,* speaking of the prayer of faith, he notes that "many
individuals, who have set themselves to examine the Bible on
this subject," have found his views correct. "They found that
God meant by his promise just what a plain, common sense man
would understand them to mean." If people approach Scripture
in a spirit of prayer for illumination, Finney held that all
converted persons could rightly interpret it:

> They are competent witnesses to this, for they have experience
> of its truth. The experimental Christian has no more need of
> external evidence to prove the truth of the Bible to his mind,
> than he has to prove his own existence. . . . The Christian is
> conscious that the Bible is true. The veriest child in religion
> knows by his own experience the truth of the Bible.

Thus Finney's belief in the authority of Scripture rested on a very pragmatic base, as did the rest of his theology and methodology: "It answers every condition perfectly; it must therefore come from God."

THE BIBLE IS THE TEXT BOOK

Phoebe Palmer likewise displayed a similar bibliocentricity in her exposition of holiness. She said of herself, "My highest and all-consuming desire was to be a Bible Christian." In almost every work by or about her, some variation of the following quotation appears:

> THE BIBLE, THE BLESSED BIBLE, IS THE TEXT BOOK. Not Wesley, not Fletcher, not Finney, not Mahan, not Upham, not Mrs. Phoebe Palmer, but the Bible—the holy BIBLE, is the first and last, and in the midst always. The BIBLE is the standard, the groundwork, the platform, the creed.

Repeatedly Palmer contended that "holiness is not the distinguishing doctrine of any sect, but the crowning doctrine of the Bible." Concerning the Tuesday Meeting, it was said, "The text-book has not been Wesley or Calvin or any human author, but always and everywhere the Bible." Palmer, as editor of the *Guide to Holiness,* counseled a letter writer:

> I fear that my dear friend has been hindered, in his Christian course, by an undue attention to the technicalities in theology. The Bible is a wonderfully simple book; and, if you had taken the naked Word of God as . . . your counsel, instead of taking the opinions of men in regard to that *Word,* you might have been a more enlightened, simple, happy and useful Christian.

Like Finney, Palmer saw an interaction between experience and Scripture. She told readers of the *Guide,* "You cannot illustrate scriptural truth more instructively or more inspiringly, than by your *personal* realizations." And she noted in a letter to the Uphams: "Surely, the excellency of a religious experience is only to be tested by its conformity to the word of God." Sarah Cooke, the Chicago exhorter who led D. L. Moody into the experience of holiness, quoted Palmer as declaring, "Were I to live to be as old as Methuselah, and to be brought into the most perplexing circumstances any one could be brought into, I should ever find the light and guidance I need in the Bible."

Guide editor George Hughes's eulogy of Sarah Lankford Palmer could just as easily have applied to her sister Phoebe:

> The fact is, this holy woman luxuriated upon the Living Word. She had no trouble about "higher" or "lower criticism." She accepted the Holy Bible in its entirety, from Genesis to Revelation, and recognized that it was her high vocation to distribute it to hungry souls.

Yet their acceptance was not a rank literalism. In *The Promise of the Father,* her 1859 defense of women's ministry, Phoebe Palmer noted that Protestants do not take literally the words of Jesus, "This is my body broken for you." Thus she found it odd that they do take literally Paul's phrase, "Let your women keep silence." Both she said were "relics of Popery."

This emphasis on the Bible and on lay, commonsense interpretations of it were important ingredients in the ecumenical base needed for the Finneyite revivals, the holiness movement, and the woman's movement. Leaders stressed repeatedly that these movements and other cooperative reforms were not sectarian movements, that they were bound by no creeds, no doctrinal confessions. They simply read the Bible for themselves and adhered to its teachings, obvious to all.

A TIME FOR REINTERPRETATION

Throughout the nineteenth century, Christian women and men wrote innumerable works questioning traditional biblical definitions of woman's role, offering quite different interpretations of the relevant texts and pointing out new passages which had not previously been considered relevant. In addition to Sarah Grimké's *Letters on the Equality of the Sexes* (1837), Antoinette Brown's article on I Corinthians 14:34-35 and I Timothy 2:11-12 in the *Oberlin Review* (July 1849), Phoebe Palmer's *The Promise of the Father* (1859), and Catherine Booth's *Female Ministry* (1859), there were other works, ranging from letters sent to be read at conventions, speeches given, and articles in journals to full-length books [see the Appendix for a partial list]. To cite just one example, the Worcester convention received a letter from Elizabeth Wilson of Cadiz, Ohio, commenting on Scripture. She authored a two-hundred-page book, *A Scriptural View of Woman's Rights and Duties* (1849).

The early nineteenth century was a time for biblical reinterpretation in general. Higher criticism was capturing the imaginations of German scholars, though outside of a few Harvard and Andover faculty members and Boston Unitarians who had studied in Europe, few Americans knew anything yet of such findings. Still, reinterpretation was being done by many people on a variety of subjects within the framework of traditional understandings of Scripture.

For one thing, the shifts in theological understanding going on among New Haven theologians previously discussed correlated with a shift in biblical understandings which benefited women. For example, the shift away from a concentration on original sin liberated women from the tyranny of past accusations. If Adam was no longer responsible for human sinfulness, then neither was Eve. The emphasis on instantaneous conversion and sanctification brought to light certain New Testament characters and events, particularly those surrounding Pentecost, which revealed women's roles in a new way.

The support which Finneyite revivalists gave various social reforms also led to new interpretations. Although scriptural arguments were not a major issue in the temperance movement, reformers certainly emphasized a different reading than had such men as Martin Luther, who saw nothing unbiblical about having a few beers. At first temperance workers asked only that people abandon the use of hard liquor; early pledges exempted beer, wine, and hard cider. But when Arthur Tappan began to advocate unfermented grape juice instead of wine at Holy Communion, he was certainly going against a literal reading of the New Testament.

More important for feminists was the reinterpretation undertaken by abolitionists. Against a literal, ahistorical understanding of Scripture which argued that whatever the

Bible displayed and declared was divine decree for all time, the abolitionists saw the Bible as a document of its times, inaugurating a new age and implementing social change as best it could in the ancient social milieu. In addition, they saw it offering guidelines for increasing social change which those with all the advantages of nineteenth-century democratic American culture were supposed to implement. Rather than as shoring up the status quo, Paul was read by abolitionists as recognizing it but undermining it. Obviously this type of thinking had great potential for application to woman's rights, as Antoinette Brown demonstrated in Cleveland in 1853:

> If we believe the Bible to endorse the institutions of patriarchal times, must we therefore suppose those institutions to be obligatory, or even right, for the present age? Not if we believe Christ, for he told us that things such as polygamy, were permitted on account of the hardness of their hearts. . . . God's will comes to us progressively, and light increases as we are ready to receive it.

ABOLITION

The epitome of the Finneyites' argument for immediate abolition was Theodore Weld's *The Bible Against Slavery* (1837). Whereas southerners were defending slavery using traditional biblical interpretations, Weld and his cohorts in the American Anti-Slavery Society pounded home the "SIN OF SLAVERY." They interpreted the Bible to condemn rather than condone slavery, often working with passages in the New Testament which lie side by side with passages concerning women's roles (e.g., Eph. 5:21–6:9; Col. 3:18–4:1; I Peter 2:13–3:7; and on the other side, Gal. 3:28). It was Theodore Weld who instructed Angelina and Sarah Grimké in revivalist methods of abolitionizing.

When the sisters were challenged about their lecturing on abolition to promiscuous assemblies in 1837, Weld suggested that they use their Quakerism as a cover. Angelina, heeding Weld's example rather than his words, replied heatedly in a letter (20 August 1837):

We are actuated by the full conviction that if we are to do any good in the Anti Slavery cause, our *right* to labor in it *must* be firmly established; *not* on the ground of Quakerism, but on the only firm basis of human rights, the Bible.

Sarah sent a similar message to another radical colleague, Henry C. Wright (12 August 1837):

I cannot consent to make my Quakerism an excuse for my exercising the rights and performing the duties of a rational and responsible being, because I claim nothing in virtue of my connection with the Society of Friends; all I claim is as a woman and for any woman whom God qualifies and commands to preach his blessed Gospel. I claim the Bible not Quakerism as my sanction and I wish this fully understood.

Angelina pleaded with Weld to stand with them on the same ground (12 August 1837):

Now we want thee to sustain us on the high ground of MORAL RIGHT, *not* of Quaker peculiarity. This question must be met *now;* let us do it as *moral* beings, and not try to turn a SECTARIAN *peculiarity* to the best account for the benefit of Abolitionism. WE do not stand on Quaker ground, but on the Bible ground and *moral right.* What we claim for ourselves, we claim for every woman whom God has called and qualified with gifts and graces.

The sisters went on to explain that while Quakers did allow women to speak under certain conditions, at least the Quakers they knew supported neither abolition nor woman's rights.

In the first of her *Letters on the Equality of the Sexes and the Condition of Woman,* written in 1837 in answer to clerical critics and especially the *Pastoral Letter* from the Massachusetts Congregational clergy, Sarah declared the Bible to be her authority:

In examining this important subject, I shall depend solely on the Bible to designate the sphere of woman, because I believe almost everything that has been written on this subject, has been the result of a misconception of the simple truths revealed in the Scriptures, in consequence of the false translation of many passages of Holy Writ.

Again, in her conclusion, she wrote, "I am aware, they [the letters] contain some new views; but I believe they are based on the immutable truths of the Bible."

THE WOMAN QUESTION

The person responsible for answering the clerical critics and their biblical arguments at the earliest woman's rights conventions was Antoinette Brown. A refrain seems to run through the accounts of those early conventions in the *History of Woman Suffrage:*

> Antoinette Louisa Brown, a graduate of Oberlin College, and a student in Theology, made a logical argument on woman's position in the Bible, claiming her complete equality with man, the simultaneous creation of the sexes, and their moral responsibilities as individual and imperative. [Worcester, Massachusetts, 1850]

> During the proceedings, Miss Brown, in a long speech on the Bible, had expounded many doctrines and passages of Scripture in regard to woman's position, in direct opposition to the truths generally promulgated by General Assemblies, and the lesser lights of the Church. [Cleveland, Ohio, 1853]

> Antoinette Brown was called on as usual to meet the Bible argument. A clergyman accused her of misapplying texts. . . . Miss Brown maintained her position. [Saratoga Springs, New York, 1855]

> Antoinette Louisa Brown had formed her idea of Woman's Rights from the Bible, and some of her friends thought that she was wasting her time in writing a treatise on Woman's Rights deduced from Scripture. [New York, New York, 1856]

Brown had studied Bible under the guidance of Finney, Mahan, Henry Cowles, and other faculty members at Oberlin. In an 18 March 1848 letter to Stone, she mentioned that she had been "examining the Bible position of woman a good deal this winter reading various commentaries, comparing them with each other and with the Bible and hunting up every passage in the Scriptures that have any bearing on the subject either near or remote."

Eventually she put down her thoughts in a paper. In her diary she reported: "Professor [John] Morgan occupied one entire class period discussing my paper, although the members of the class said they could not see that either of us had made the matter plainer or settled the question." Evidently the paper became the talk of the school because in her own reminiscences of Oberlin, she reported:

> President Mahan was in office for two years after I entered college. He was liberal; and criticized on that account. I used to air my pet opinions in my compositions and one of them was an exegesis on S. Paul's teachings—Suffer not women to speak in the Church. President Mahan heard of it and sent for it and had it printed in the next edition of the *Oberlin Review* [July 1849]. . . . Prof. Fairchild rather objected and wrote an article on the other side. It was printed in the same number.

A leading graduate pastoring in the area supported Brown's position in the following issue.

Brown was not the only one to reinterpret the Bible and use it as authority for the early woman's rights movement. At the first national convention in Worcester, Abby H. Price of Hopedale, Massachusetts, gave a lengthy speech on the subject. The convention also received a letter from Jane Cowen of Logansport, Indiana, in which she declared:

> After studying on woman's position for 15 years, without divulging my thoughts to any person, taking the Bible for my guide, I have come to the conclusion that this great evil has its original root in the Church of God. . . . I am of the opinion, that if the Church would allow women the privileges that God has given her, in both the Old and New Testaments, and education equal with the male sex, every right that belongs to her would follow.

At Philadelphia in 1854, Hannah Tracy Cutler debated biblical questions with a minister. She declared:

> The time has come for woman to read and interpret Scripture for herself. . . . It is a pity that those who would recommend the Bible as the revealed will of the all-wise and benevolent Creator, should uniformly quote it on the side of tyranny and oppression. I think we owe it to our religion and ourselves to wrest it from

such hands, and proclaim the beautiful spirit breathed through
all its commands and precepts, instead of dwelling so much on
isolated texts that have no application in our day and generation.

Caroline Cowles, a Canandaigua, New York, schoolgirl,
heard Quaker Susan B. Anthony (1820–1906) speak in 1854
and recorded in her diary:

When I told Grandmother about it, she said she guessed Susan
B. Anthony had forgotten that St. Paul said women should keep
silence. I told her, no, she didn't for she spoke particularly about
St. Paul and said if he had lived in these times . . . he would have
been as anxious to have women at the head of government as she
was. I could not make Grandmother agree with her at all.

At an 1869 convention in Milwaukee, Stanton had both aid
and opposition from clergy. Reports Stanton:

The platform . . . was graced with several reverend gentlemen
. . . all of whom maintained woman's equality with eloquence
and fervor. The Bible was discussed from Genesis to
Revelation, in all its bearings on the question under consideration. By special request I gave my Bible argument which was
published in full in the daily papers. A Rev. Mr. Love, who took
the opposite view . . . criticized some of my Hebrew
translations, and scientific expositions, but as the rest of the
learned D.D.s sustained my views, I shall rest in the belief that
bro. Love, with time and thought, will come to the same
conclusions.

Some, however, remained unconvinced. The *Syracuse Star*
commented in 1852: "The women of the Tomfoolery Convention, now being held in this city, talk as fluently of the Bible and
God's teachings in their speeches as if they could draw an
argument from inspiration in maintenance of their woman's
rights stuff."

To the end of her life, Lucy Stone retained her confidence
that the Bible, rightly interpreted, supported woman's rights,
according to Alice Stone Blackwell. Once on a speaking tour,
Stone found herself sharing an Ohio riverboat with a minister
who began to argue with her about women's headcoverings.
Losing the argument, he told her she should study Scripture

more diligently. She shocked him into silence by saying, "I have studied them in their original. I have read them in Greek and can translate them for you." She went on to explain various Greek words. By the time the boat docked she had shown that he was utterly ignorant of the Greek himself and not very well versed in the English Bible.

SCRIPTURAL DEFENSES

The women developed several different arguments, both defensive and offensive, based on the Bible to use against their critics, clerical and lay. Defensively, they became expert in listing women who played prominent roles in spiritual and political life in Bible times: Deborah, Miriam, Huldah, Jael, Anna, Priscilla, Phoebe. They never tired of pointing to the example of Jesus' attitude toward women. They knew that the King James translators had done all women a disservice by calling Phoebe in Romans 16:1-2 a servant when Paul called her a deacon or minister. They were quick to point out all of the other women whom Paul also designates as his co-workers in spreading the gospel.

The women also had ready arguments to counter traditional interpretations of "Let your women keep silence in the churches" (I Cor. 14:34), which was used against women's speaking in any public forum. Brown had outlined the rebuttal to that in her *Oberlin Review* article. She noted that few traditionalists took the prohibition as literally as they claimed. They let women sing in church, pray at family altars, and teach Sabbath schools. She argued that the passage in question commanded women only to cease chattering in public meetings but did not prohibit edifying discourse such as prayers, prophesying, preaching, and teaching. Concerning I Timothy 2:11-12 ("Let the woman learn in silence with all subjection. But I suffer not a woman to teach, nor to usurp authority over the man, but to be in silence"), Brown pointed out that the crucial word was *usurp,* which meant to dictate or to take to oneself authority which was not given. Thus a woman could be duly ordained or licensed to preach, could be given authority by the church. In her speeches Brown argued that in the Garden of

Eden, God did not say that the husband "shall" rule over the wife (Gen. 3:16), but that he "will." God would not command anyone to commit an intrinsically evil act, said Brown, reflecting the New Divinity's efforts to avoid any theology which would make God the author of sin.

The women also developed several new arguments. One was based simply on the Golden Rule. Angelina Grimké used it in regard to slavery in 1829 when she asked a friend in Charleston if she would wish to be a slave. When the woman answered no, Angelina suggested that she should not own slaves then. Antoinette appealed to the same source in Cleveland in 1853: "I claim that this movement is preeminently a great christian movement. It is founded in the christian doctrine 'Thou shalt love the Lord thy God supremely, and thy neighbor as thyself'; and the Golden Rule of the new gospel."

One of women's favorite texts was Galatians 3:28, "There is neither Jew nor Greek, there is neither bond nor free, there is neither male nor female: for ye are all one in Christ Jesus." Used frequently by abolitionists, its application to woman's rights was obvious. Many made it the keystone of their hermeneutic, arguing that it represented the epitome of how relationships should be in Christ's millennial kingdom. Almost all writers on woman's rights were also familiar with Methodist biblical scholar Adam Clarke's comment on it: "Under the blessed spirit of Christianity, [women] have equal *rights,* equal *privileges,* and equal *blessings;* and, let me add, they are equally *useful.*"

Another argument highly developed in this era was the pentecostal argument. The title of Palmer's book referred to it: *The Promise of the Father; or, a Neglected Speciality of the Last Days.* She also wrote a tract entitled *The Tongue of Fire on the Daughters of the Lord.* Text for the argument is found in Peter's speech at the founding of the church in Jerusalem on Pentecost. In Acts 2:17-18 he quoted the prophecy of Joel:

> And it shall come to pass in the last days, saith God, I will pour out of my Spirit upon all flesh: and your sons and your daughters shall prophesy, and your young men shall see visions, and your old men shall dream dreams:

And on my servants and on my handmaidens I will pour out in those days of my Spirit; and they shall prophesy.

With sarcasm Palmer asked rhetorically if anyone seriously thought that when the twelve apostles saw the tongues of fire fall on their sisters, they called a session or vestry meeting to vote on whether or not their sisters should be allowed to speak! Time and time again the women quoted Acts 2:4, always with the same emphasis: "They were *all* filled with the Holy Ghost, and began to speak. . . ." Women admitted that women had been denied their rights in the past but argued that the age of change had arrived. As early as 1856, Palmer was drafting parts of her book, and she wrote in her diary:

The dispensation of the Spirit is now entered upon,—the last dispensation previous to the last glorious appearing of our Lord and Saviour Jesus Christ. . . . Male and female are now one in Christ Jesus. The Spirit now descended alike on all. And they were *all* filled with the Holy Ghost, and began to speak as the Spirit gave utterance.

In her book she exclaimed:

What a resurrection of power we shall witness in the church, when, in a sense answerable to the original design of God, women shall come forth, a very great army, engaging in all holy activities; when, in the true scriptural sense, and answerable to the design of the God of the Bible, women shall become the "help meet" to man's spiritual nature.

This argument embodied the Finneyite understanding of conversion and perfection as more than legal justification. It affirmed that Christians were not only justified before God but were also regenerate, reborn, made new, capable of being restored to the Edenic state. For women it made possible the sweeping away of centuries of patriarchal, misogynist culture in the instant of conversion. The argument that "this is the way we've always done it" holds no power for someone for whom "all things have been made new." Said the women of the Boston Female Anti-Slavery Society in 1837: "What is the sphere and duty of woman, it rests with each one for herself to determine; and to do this, she is aided by a revelation which it rests with each one for herself to interpret!"

THERE IS NO NEED FOR ANY WRITTEN AUTHORITY

The reinterpretation of the Bible in regard to woman's rights was carried on with fervor throughout the nineteenth century and into our own. The early volumes of the *History of Woman Suffrage* contain ample information concerning the debates, but the movement then very consciously turned away from them. The turning point came at the conventions in Syracuse in 1852 and Cleveland in 1853. Brown had put heart and soul into the struggle to answer the critics. She proposed a resolution in Syracuse:

> *Resolved,* That the Bible recognizes the rights, duties and privileges of Woman as a public teacher as every way equal with those of man; that it enjoins upon her no subjection that is not enjoined upon him; and that it truly and practically recognizes neither male nor female in Christ Jesus.

She defended the resolution in a lengthy, closely argued speech. But other, older leaders in the movement were tired of the seemingly endless discussions of the same old issues. After two days of debate fueled by harangues from visiting clergymen, Ernestine Rose, a Polish Jew, declared:

> For my part, I see no need to appeal to any written authority, particularly when it is so obscure and indefinite as to admit of different interpretations. When the inhabitants of Boston converted their harbor into a teapot rather than submit to unjust taxes, they did not go to the Bible for their authority; for if they had, they would have been told from the same authority to "give unto Caesar what belonged to Caesar." Had the people when they rose in the might of their right to throw off the British yoke, appealed to the Bible for authority, it would have answered them, "Submit to the powers that be, for they are from God." No! on Human Rights and Freedom, on the subject that is as self-evident as that two and two make four, there is no need for any written authority.

In an effort to make peace, Quaker elder Lucretia Mott abandoned her chair as president and spoke in opposition to Brown's resolution. She recalled her experiences in trying to refute proslavery arguments based on the Bible. She said that some abolitionists had learned the futility of trying to match biblical arguments and finally "to adhere to their own great work—that of declaring the inherent right of man to himself and his earnings—and that self-evident truth needed no argument or outward authority." She moved that the resolution therefore be tabled, which it was.

A very similar debate ensued the next year, 1853, in Cleveland. Again Brown put forth her position. Though conceding perhaps wifely submission, Mahan defended the Bible and his former student's interpretations. But again Rose stood to rebuke Brown:

> "There is a time and a season for everything," and this is no time to discuss the Bible. I appeal to the universal experience of men, to sustain me, in asking whether the introduction of Theological quibbles, has not been a firebrand wherever they have been thrown? We have a political question under discussion; let us take that question and argue it with reference to right and wrong.

And so the discussion ended and the movement moved in a more secular direction, concentrating on more strictly political goals and principles.

One wonders what might have happened if the feminists had instead followed the example of the abolitionists, who built their movement on the conviction that slaveholding was not only a violation of a person's political rights but morally sinful. What would have happened if nineteenth-century feminists had called sexism sin in an age which still believed in the concept? Their reinterpretations of the Bible gave them a base from which to confront antifeminism at its roots, but some of them chose to abandon it.

CHAPTER 7

THE UNCTION MAKES
THE PREACHER

*Set women to praying? Why, the next thing, I
suppose, will be to set them to preaching!*
                                    —*One of Finney's critics*

*O*sie Fitzgerald of Bernardsville, New Jersey, was converted at age fifteen in an 1828 revival at the local Presbyterian church. When a noted holiness evangelist visited the Methodist church in Newark in 1856, she sought entire sanctification. The Spirit of God first asked if she would surrender her children to God, then her husband, and then all her property. Each one she "laid on the altar," yet she did not experience holiness.

Finally the Spirit asked, "If I give you a clean heart, and sanctify you wholly, will you speak before this people and tell them what I have done for you?" Having been brought up a Presbyterian, she explained: "I was very much opposed to women speaking in the church. I thought no one but a bold Methodist woman would speak in church." Consequently she said, "No; it is not the place for a female to speak." Again the question was repeated. She replied: "I will do it if the Lord requires it, but He does not, for there are plenty of men to speak." Her agony of soul only increased.

Finally she surrendered all: "Yes, Lord, though it be before a thousand people." Immediately she received the witness of the Spirit to her sanctification. Soon she felt led to pray in a meeting, but she hesitated until it was too late. "What but a man-fearing or a man-pleasing spirit prevented you?" the Spirit chided. She subsequently prayed in public and even preached.

Fitzgerald's was a common story in revivalism and the holiness movement. The Puritans, along with their Presbyterian, Congregationalist, and Episcopalian descendants, gloried in the authority of a learned clergy. In the nineteenth century the ministry, along with many other occupations, was becoming professionalized. Finney's opponents, Beecher and Nettleton, along with most Presbygational ministers of their generation, were college graduates—Yale in their case. Ministers of the next generation were to attend seminary as well. In addition to Harvard, Yale, and Princeton colleges, there were already Andover, Princeton, Hartford, and Auburn seminaries. Finney himself represented the last generation to be trained by reading law or reading for the ministry within main-line denominations. Within revivalism he continued that legacy. Finney said he was offered a scholarship to study at Princeton but declined it. George Gale said in his memoirs that he attempted unsuccessfully to get Finney financial aid at Princeton, Andover, and Auburn. Whatever the case, Finney represented and shaped a different concept of ministry.

Except for his tenure as pastor of First Congregational Church in Oberlin, Finney never served an extended time as a settled pastor. He was a revivalist, an itinerant. He was often invited into a church by a group of laypeople currently without a pastor or by people who wanted to start a revival in a church they considered dead. Many were women. Finney constantly encouraged laypeople to challenge theological authorities, ecclesiastical leaders, and church administrators. For example, he told of one young woman from "a very wicked family" who, after conversion, expressed concern about older church members' theology which seemed to question God's readiness to act. At first her pastor tried to reason with her theologically, but then he read his Bible, learned she was correct, preached the new truth, and awakened instant revival. Another woman in New Jersey was positive her church was ready for a revival, but the minister would not hold any meetings. So she hired a carpenter, had seats made, and invited people to her house. Again instant revival ensued.

SOUL WINNERS

Finney was convinced that "a minister may be *very learned and not wise*" because "the end of the ministry is the salvation of the soul" and "the amount of [a minister's] wisdom is to be decided, . . . by the *number* of cases in which he is successful in converting sinners." This definition of ministry—divorced from intellectual leadership, social authority, sacramental power, and moral discipline—opened the door to women, who were being culturally defined anyway as the keepers of religious values. Finney concluded a lecture on "A Wise Minister Will Be Successful" with the call: "Men—women—you are bound to be wise in winning souls." In another sermon, entitled "Converting Sinners a Christian Duty," he declared, "Each one, male or female, of every age, and in any position in life whatsoever, should make it a business to save souls."

Women saw the implications clearly. Lucy Stone asked repeatedly why,

> when Antoinette Brown felt that she was commanded to preach, and to arrest the progress of thousands that were on the road to hell; why, when she applied for ordination they acted as though they had rather the whole world should go to hell, than that Antoinette Brown should be allowed to tell them how to keep out of it?

When the Massachusetts General Association of Congregational Ministers attempted to outline the limits of women's ministry to the Grimké sisters in their *Pastoral Letter* by suggesting that women lead inquirers to pastors for instruction, Sarah replied rather hotly:

> Now this is assuming that all pastors are better qualified to give instruction than women. This I utterly deny. . . . The Lord Jesus says,—"Come unto me and learn of me." He points his followers to no man; and when woman is made the favored instrument of rousing a sinner to his lost and helpless condition, she has no right to substitute any teacher for Christ; . . . More souls have probably been lost by going down to Egypt for help, and by trusting in man in the early stages of religious experience, than by any other error. . . . The business of men and women, who are ORDAINED OF GOD to preach the unsearchable riches of Christ to a lost and perishing world, is to lead souls to Christ, and not to Pastors for instruction.

As we have said, Finney started from his own experience. The revival in which he was converted was led by Jedediah Burchard and his wife. It was she who organized circles of women for prayer. Finney's legal training shaped his sermonizing more in the form of a lawyer's summation for the jury. Thus his language was colloquial, his illustrations pungent, his arguments pointed. In his *Lectures on Revivals,* Finney advised ministers "to do as the lawyer does when he wants to make a jury understand him perfectly. He uses a style perfectly colloquial." His earliest experience was as a missionary for the female missionary society, working a territory where churches were often without pastors. He began holding protracted meetings in 1825, preaching every evening and three times on Sunday. One of his early associates was Father Daniel Nash, who was a great believer in and practitioner of agonized public prayer. People said one could hear him for miles. And he was not afraid to be explicit about which sinners needed the Lord's touch. It was Nash who organized women to pray for their unconverted husbands. He also organized the holy bands of laypeople who visited house to house, inviting people to the meetings, inquiring about the state of souls. Women took a leading role, especially at Utica in 1826. There Finney adopted the practice of holding anxious meetings for those concerned about the state of their soul. The anxious bench became a regular part of his meetings in Rochester in 1830. During this time Finney was an evangelist for the Oneida Evangelical Association, which he and friends founded in December 1826.

Many of these practices had been adapted from Methodist usage. The goal of all of Finney's new measures was simply "to get the attention of the people, and bring them to listen to the truth." The criterion was success: "When the blessing evidently follows the introduction of the *measure itself,* the proof is unanswerable, that the measure is wise."

A CONTROVERSIAL PRACTICE

Finney's revivals soon came under fire from local Unitarians and Universalists, but neither seemed particularly concerned about women's activities. Finney's friends replied in 1826 with a *Narrative of the Revival of Religion in the County of Oneida.*

Among the thirteen "Means Which Appear to Have Been Blessed in Promoting These Revivals" they listed women praying. Eastern critics Nettleton and Beecher, however, were particularly outraged by it. Nettleton noted that the revivalists apparently took perverse delight in getting "females to pray in school houses and circles where men, and *ministers especially* are present to see and *hear* them pray for them and others by name." He wrote:

> Whoever introduces the practice of females praying in promiscuous assemblies,—let the practice once become general,—will ere long find to his sorrow, that he has made an inlet to other denominations, and entailed an everlasting quarrel in those churches generally.

Beecher too was shocked at the idea of "female prayer in promiscuous assemblies" and termed it the greatest "evil to be apprehended," fearing it would "disrobe the female mind of those ornaments of sensibility, and clothe it with the rough texture of masculine fibre." Conservative William Weeks in his critical *Pastoral Letter of the Ministers of the Oneida Association,* among twenty-nine "Evils to Be Guarded Against," cited "allowing anybody and everybody to speak and pray in promiscuous meetings of whatever age, sex, or qualification." At New Lebanon the two sides were able to reach agreement on everything except whether or not it was "right for a woman to pray in the presence of men." Beecher argued that the practice was "unscriptural and inadmissable." Finney's men replied with arguments "manifestly too conclusive to admit of any refutation," at least according to Finney.

Despite the criticism, Finney continued to champion the right of women to pray and speak, and to encourage them to do so. In his 1835 *Lectures on Revivals of Religion,* he said it was most desirable in prayer meetings to "give the meeting to the Spirit of God," to let anyone pray who felt led to do so, rather than to call on specific people. He said there should be numerous prayer meetings so "as to exercise the gifts of every individual member of the church—male and female." In an 1845 issue of the *Oberlin Evangelist,* he replied to a question from a Miss A. E. of Vermont, who asked how she should react when she felt an impulse to speak in a public meeting or was requested to do so. He acknowledged that "some have supposed that the Scriptures plainly prohibit the speaking or praying of women in promiscuous assemblies," but said, "I do not so understand the teachings of the Bible." He counseled her to check her impulses to certify that they came from the Spirit and not Satan, and to be guided by circumstances, but "if benevolence manifestly requires you to speak or pray anywhere, at any time, your duty is plain."

A RIGHT TO BE DEFENDED

The right to speak publicly was a right which required constant defense. Weld advised the Grimké sisters simply to say nothing of rights and keep on speaking. Had their topic been less controversial, it might have worked, but they realized that "if then we 'give *no reason* for the hope that is in us,' that we have *equal rights* with our brethren, how can we expect to be permitted *much longer to exercise those rights?"* Cried Angelina to Weld (20 August 1837):

> We *must* meet it, and meet it *now* and meet it like *women* in the fear of the Lord. . . . They utterly deny *our right* to interfere with this or any other moral reform except in the particular way *they* choose to mark out for us to walk in. . . . Why, my dear brothers, can you not see the deep laid scheme of the clergy against us as lecturers? They know full well that if they can persuade the people it is a *shame* for us to speak in public, and that every time we open our mouths for the dumb we are breaking a divine command, . . . we should have *no hearers.* . . . If we surrender the right to *speak* to the public this year, we must surrender the right to petition next year and the right to *write* the year after that and so on.

The subject of woman's right to speak in public was a controversial one, even at Oberlin, and Finney's position in the faculty discussions is unclear. In 1838 the principal of the Ladies' Department, Mrs. Alice Welch Cowles, wrote in her diary: "God will not lead me to *speak* or instruct assemblies because, if I mistake not, he has told me with other females, not to do so." Yet the second Mrs. Cowles, Minerva Dayton

Penfield, Josephine Bateham's mother, presided at an 1853 temperance convention in Columbus. Henry Cowles was still saying in the 1859 *Oberlin Evangelist* that women could not speak in large assemblies "without violating the natural sense of propriety which God has given us, or the real sense of scripture." In the 1840s President Mahan and Professor James Thome supported women's right to participate in coeducational rhetoric classes and even began one in 1839, but the women petitioned to be excused, more shy than those who followed. Stone and Brown begged Thome to let them debate, which he did once, but this brought down the wrath of the Ladies' Board. The women had to organize their own debating society in the woods.

Both Brown and Stone began to lecture in neighboring towns. On 1 August 1846 Stone gave a speech at a celebration of the anniversary of the emancipation of West Indian slaves. Called on the carpet by the Ladies' Board, she was asked by Mary Mahan if she were not "embarrassed and frightened" to be exposed on a platform with all those men. Stone replied that those men were President Mahan and her professors, and she was not a bit afraid of them. Mahan worked hard to obtain for Stone and for his own daughter Anna the privilege of reading their own graduation papers in 1847 and 1848, but the faculty refused. Stone, therefore, refused to write one.

During the term when Brown began her theological studies, Finney led a meeting one evening in which all new theological students were asked one by one to testify to their religious experience and call to the ministry. When someone suggested it was Brown's turn, he looked surprised and, thinking her a visitor, remarked, "Oh, the women, we don't ask them to speak now." She left in tears, and then someone explained to Finney that she was not a visitor but a student. He apologized and said, "Oh, of course, then, she must tell us why she wishes to become a minister." Brown reported that "he called upon me on the next similar occasion and from that time on no one could have been more helpful or more considerate in making my position both easy and satisfactory than Professor Finney." She explained that he had been away when the faculty had debated her admission. At first Finney did not call on Brown for class devotions as he did male students, perhaps assuming that she, like other women students, did not wish to participate. Again another student informed him she was hurt, so one day when he met her on the street he exclaimed: "Antoinette, you may pray! You shall *pray*! I did not know you wanted to pray!" She participated regularly after that. Finney had a practice in another class of drawing students' names out of a hat and asking them to discourse extemporaneously on whatever topic was at hand. Brown's name came up so often that other students complained that Finney was playing favorites. Finney's first wife, Lydia, reportedly discouraged Brown from her aspirations, but "the second Mrs. Finney was very liberal and said—'Antoinette, always follow your own convictions.' "

HAVING A CALL

The bedrock of a set-apart ministry for the revivalists and for women was simply having a "call." Brown reported that "when President [*sic*] Finney heard me give my reasons for wanting to become a minister he said that some women had been called to preach and I might be of that number." Indeed, it was this sense of call which gave women the courage to step into ministerial roles. As Sarah Grimké wrote in her *Letters on Equality:*

> It is truly marvellous that any woman can rise above the pressure of circumstances which combine to crush her. Nothing can strengthen her to do this in the character of a preacher of righteousness, but a call from Jehovah himself. And when the voice of God penetrates the deep recesses of her heart, and commands her to go and cry in the ears of the people, she is ready to exclaim, "Ah, Lord God, behold I cannot speak, for I am a woman.["] I have known women in different religious societies, who have felt like the prophet. "His word was in my heart as a burning fire shut up in my bones, and I was weary with forbearing." But they have not dared to open their lips, and have endured all the intensity of suffering, produced by disobedience to God, rather than encounter heartless ridicule and injurious suspicions. I rejoice that we have been the oppressed, rather than the oppressors.

Sarah spoke from experience, for she herself had felt called to the public ministry and had been continually discouraged by Quaker elders.

Methodist women particularly were inspired by a litany of foremothers. They were well aware that John Wesley, as an Anglican priest, did not favor lay or woman preachers until his mother, Susanna, set him straight: "I charge you before God, take care what you do, for that man is as truly called of God to preach the gospel as ever you were!" Susanna herself had held prayer meetings and taught her neighbors in Epworth, despite her husband Samuel's objections. Both Palmer and Willard quote a letter from Wesley to Mary Bosanquet Fletcher in which he wrote, "My Dear Sister,—I think the strength of the cause rests here—in your having an *extraordinary* call. So I am persuaded had every one of our lay preachers; otherwise I could not countenance his preaching at all." Palmer quoted another Methodist leader as counseling a woman "on whose head the tongue of fire had fallen": "Your call is of God; I would have you go in at every open door, but do not wait till the door is thrown open wide; go in if it be on the jar." Barbara Heck (1734–1804) had done just that in founding the first Methodist class meetings and churches in the United States (1766) and in Canada (1785).

Palmer was confident of her own call:

> That God has called me to stand before the people, and proclaim His truth, has long been beyond question. So fully has God made my commission known to my own soul, and so truly has He set His seal upon it, before the upper and lower world, in the conversion of thousands of precious souls, and the sanctification of a multitude of believers, that even Satan does not seem to question that my call is divine.

Thus her conception of the minister's task coincided with Finney's. She never applied for nor was she given any kind of preaching license, but as one eulogist noted: "Her license came from no subordinate source. She was accredited from on high. Her authority and credentials were conferred by the Holy Ghost. She was set apart and gifted as a gentle leader. . . . She was vested with a remarkable power to produce immediate results." This was the type of "ordination" she urged on other women in *Faith and Its Effects:*

> And now, my dear sister, do not be startled, when I tell you that you have been *ordained* for a great work. Not by the imposition

of moral hands, or a call from man. No, Christ, the great Head of the church, hath chosen you, "and ordained you, that ye should go and bring forth fruit." O my sister, yours is indeed a high and holy calling. Alas for you, if you are not found faithful to the trust committed!

DO NOT QUENCH THE SPIRIT

To resist such a call was to risk damnation. Palmer's biographer, Richard Wheatley, put it clearly: "It is always right to obey the Holy Spirit's command, and if that is laid upon a woman, to preach the Gospel, then it is right for her to do so; it is a duty that she cannot neglect without falling into condemnation." Palmer, in *Promise of the Father,* tells the story of Sarah Mallet (Boyce), a friend of John Wesley's. For some years she felt called to preach but resisted. Then one day she fell into a fit in which she thought herself to be in another town preaching. Over a period of a year or so, she had eighteen such spells until she yielded to the Spirit and began preaching in reality. She was never again troubled by such fits. Wesley finally gave her a letter in 1787, stating: "We give the right hand of fellowship to Sarah Mallet, and have no objection to her being a preacher in our connection, so long as she preaches the Methodist doctrine, and attends to our discipline."

A small pamphlet, *A Scriptural Vindication of Female Preaching, Prophesying, or Exhortation,* published in this period by a woman in Oneida County, told of a similar struggle. When Deborah Peirce first experienced conversion, she felt constrained to tell others but hesitated, "knowing I had spoken much against those females that attempted to speak in public." Eventually she found the courage to speak, only to be rebuked by church leaders. So she desisted, but this led to backsliding and loss of spiritual power. After two years of agony, she returned to the place where she had first felt the Spirit's urgings, began to exhort sinners to repentance, and immediately felt at peace. But again she was opposed and so refrained. This time she felt she had committed the unpardonable sin of quenching the Holy Spirit. Nothing could restore her sense of communion with God. She studied Scripture again on the issue, and "when I found it was practiced and approved of in the old and new testament, and declared it should be in the latter days, I saw I was without excuse." Her conscience accused her of "the murdering of souls" and such horror filled her heart that she was even tempted to suicide. Eventually she found peace again when she gave her "soul up wholly to do and suffer the will of God."

Women often expressed their call in terms of a dream or vision. Maggie Newton Van Cott (1830–1914) dreamed she was in her local church when a voice said, "You must preach." In the dream she finally stepped out of her pew, went into the pulpit, and preached. Later in the dream she asked who the small, white-haired gentleman sitting near the altar was, and she was told it was John Wesley! Jarena Lee (b. 1783), a preacher in the African Methodist Episcopal Church, heard a voice in a vision which said, "Go preach the Gospel!" The next night she had a dream in which she "took a text and preached." Amanda Berry Smith saw a vision while sitting in church. She saw two letters, *G* and *O,* and heard the voice of God saying, "Go preach." The literature is replete with stories of women whose calls to minister were similarly vivid and distinct.

Is it any wonder, then, that the women of Seneca Falls in 1848 in their list of grievances complained of their "exclusion from the ministry" and declared that man "has usurped the prerogative of Jehovah himself, claiming it as his right to assign for her a sphere of action, when that belongs to her conscience and to her God"?

This different view of ministry and the place of ordination was perhaps best articulated by Wesleyan Methodist Luther Lee (1800–89) in his 1853 ordination sermon for Antoinette Brown:

> There are in the world, and there may be among us, false views
> of the nature and object of ordination. I do not believe that any
> special or specific form of ordination is necessary to constitute a
> gospel minister. We are not here to make a minister. It is not to
> confer on this, our sister, a right to preach the gospel. If she has
> not that right already, we have not power to communicate it to
> her. Nor have we met to qualify her for the work of the ministry.
> If God and mental and moral culture have not already qualified
> her, we cannot by anything we may do by way of ordaining or
> setting her apart. Nor can we, by imposition of our hands, confer

on her any special grace for the work of the ministry, or will our hands if imposed upon her head, serve as a special medium for the communication of the Holy Ghost . . . ; such ideas belong not to our theory, but are related to other systems and darker ages. All we are here to do, and all we expect to do, is, in due form, and by a solemn and impressive service, to subscribe our testimony to the fact, that in our belief, our sister in Christ, Antoinette L. Brown, is one of the ministers of the New Covenant, authorized, qualified, and called of God to preach the gospel of his Son Jesus Christ.

As John Fletcher once said, "The unction makes the preacher."

THE QUESTION OF ORDINATION

With this new understanding of the ministry, many women proceeded to join the ranks of the profession. Scriptural defenses of woman's right to preach the gospel proliferated throughout the century (see the Appendix). And for the first time in modern history, women asked for and received full ordination.

Usually honored as the first is Antoinette Louisa Brown, ordained 15 September 1853 by the First Congregational Church of Butler and Savannah, Wayne County, New York (the church had been Presbyterian but "leading members had become liberalized so much that they withdrew and became congregational"). The service was an ecumenical one—held in the Baptist church because it was larger, with the sermon given by Wesleyan Methodist Luther Lee and the charge delivered by Presbyterian Gerrit Smith. Brown's Unitarian friend Samuel J. May stayed away lest his presence imply heterodoxy.

The next ordination of record was that of Olympia Brown (Willis) (1835–1926) to the Universalist clergy in June 1863 in Malone, New York. Both Browns were active workers for temperance and woman's rights throughout their lives. Their example led to a number of ordinations within the Unitarian and Universalist denominations but only a limited number in other main-line groups. Olympia Brown ordained Phoebe Hanaford (1829–1921), another active reformer. I have found no record of another woman being ordained by either Congregationalists or Presbyterians, though Matilda Gage

mentions the ordination of five women as deacons in August
1869 by the First Presbyterian Church of Philadelphia. Anna
Oliver and Anna Howard Shaw, of course, requested full
ordination from the Methodist Episcopal Church in 1880 and
were denied. Shaw was then ordained by the Methodist
Protestants. Among the Disciples a controversy arose in 1883
over the ordination of three missionary wives along with their
husbands. Apparently the first woman ordained for the home
ministry was Clara Celestia Hall in 1888.

Among the groups teaching holiness, however, the ordination of women was rather widespread. Women appear to have
been fully ordained among the Wesleyan Methodists as early as
the 1860s. B. T. Roberts, founder of the Free Methodists,
argued on behalf of women's ordination in church conferences
of the 1860s and in his 1891 book, *Ordaining Women.* The
church licensed women as local preachers from 1873 on and had
many women leaders but did not grant full ordination until
1974. The revivalist Scandinavian groups which eventually
became the Evangelical Free Church in America ordained
women in the 1890s. Women were ordained in such Holiness
and Pentecostal denominations as the Salvation Army
(founded in 1865), Church of God (Anderson, Indiana, 1880),
Primitive Methodist Church (1889), Pentecostal Holiness
Church (1895), Pilgrim Holiness Church (1897, now merged
with the Wesleyan Methodist Church), Pillar of Fire (1901),
Church of the Nazarene (1908), and the Assemblies of God
(1914).

Ordination was then, as now, a key issue concerning woman's
place within ecclesiastical power structures, though few of the
women saw it. One who did was Sarah Grimké. In her reply to
Weld's bragging about his encouraging women to pray and testify
in revivals, she cut through to the heart of the issue:

> I do not think women being *permitted* to pray and tell their
> experience in revivals is any proof that Christians do not think it
> wrong for women to preach. This is the touchstone, to presume
> to teach the brethren. Let a woman who has prayed in a revival
> claim to be the appointed minister of Jesus and to exercise that
> office by teaching regularly on the sabbath, and she will at once
> be regarded as a fanatic, or a fool.

In her *Letters on the Equality of the Sexes,* she raised the question of why women were permitted to teach in Sabbath schools, sing in choirs, and work for benevolent causes, and yet were prohibited from officially preaching. Why? asked Sarah:

> Simply, as I believe, because in the one case we subserve *their* views and *their* interests, and act *in subordination to them;* whilst in the other, we come in contact with their interests, and claim to be on an equality with them in the highest and most important trust ever committed to man[kind], namely, the ministry of the word. It is manifest that if women were permitted to be ministers of the gospel, as they unquestionably were in the primitive ages of the Christian church, it would interfere materially with the present organized system of spiritual power and ecclesiastical authority, which is now vested solely in the hands of men.

Both Grimkés saw clearly that the issue was one of social status and power.

One has only to read the cries of their clerical critics to know they were right. Wailed one reverend gentleman: "The question is not in regard to *ability,* but to *decency,* to order, to Christian propriety." Bemoaned another: "What a sad wreck of female loveliness is she then! She can hardly conceive how ridiculous she appears in the eyes of all sober, discreet, judicious Christian men, or how great the reproach she brings upon her sex."

Their opponents saw the church as an institution based on covenant, establishment, or sacrament to be guarded and defended; the Finneyites and holiness advocates saw the church as a voluntary association of believers bound together by their religious experiences. This led them to establish "free" or "abolition" churches. The First Free Presbyterian Church was officially established 27 June 1830 when Finneyite Joel Parker moved from Rochester to New York City to become its pastor. Finney's first real pastorate was Chatham Chapel, the Second Free Presbyterian Church. The revivalists eventually formed their own Third Presbytery so they could refuse membership to those who would not sign temperance pledges or support immediate abolition. From Chatham, Finney moved in 1836 to the Sixth Free Church, Broadway Tabernacle.

Women saw this as a model to be imitated, though their

efforts never really materialized. Brown sought to use part of a bequest in 1858 to found a free church where she could "preach woman's rights with the gospel." Among Susan B. Anthony's "many schemes for regenerating the world" was one to sponsor such a church in Rochester. In 1859 she hired Corinthian Hall for Sunday evenings. Brown was one of a series of speakers who each preached for a month that year.

Frances Willard toyed with the idea off and on for many years. As early as 1877 she had spoken of "the germ of a new church in which, as Christ declared, there shall be neither male nor female." In 1883 she had noted that "while I steadfastly believe that there is no place too good for a woman to occupy, and nothing too sacred for her to do, I am not willing to go on record as a misanthropic complainer against the church which I prefer above my chief joy."

However, she and others began to discuss the possibility of a "church union," possibly reminiscent of the union church her parents attended, in which all could be members who subscribed to the Apostles' Creed and to a pledge of abstinence and social purity. In her 1888 presidential address she declared:

> The time will come, however, and not many years from now, when if representation is still denied us, it will be our solemn duty to raise once more the cry, "Here I stand, I can do no other," and step out into the larger liberty of a religious movement, where majorities and not minorities, determine the fitness of women as delegates, and where the laying on of hands in consecration, as was undoubtedly done in the early church, shall be decreed on a basis of "gifts, graces and usefulness," irregardless of sex.

Despite her disappointments, however, Willard never left the church of her choice.

"MANY WOMEN CARRIED THE NEWS"

While full ordination was comparatively rare, a great multitude of women functioned as preachers or evangelists, with or without licenses. Palmer, Willard, Whitall Smith, Amanda Berry Smith are obvious examples. Palmer's converts numbered twenty-five thousand. The first woman officially licensed by the Methodist church was Maggie Newton Van Cott in 1869. Her converts numbered seventy-five thousand. Another early Methodist was Amanda Way (1828–1914). Born a birthright Quaker in Winchester, Indiana, she was an active Methodist for twenty years and was licensed to preach in 1871. When all licenses were rescinded in 1880, she returned to being a Quaker. She was active in abolition and was founder of woman's rights activity in Indiana.

Laura Haviland (1808–98), also a birthright Quaker, became a Wesleyan Methodist preacher in 1844. She served in Michigan, where she founded the Raisin Institute for free blacks "on the Oberlin plan," until 1872 when she returned to her Quaker heritage.

Lydia Sexton was the first woman licensed as "an approved preacher" by the United Brethren Church, a German Methodist body, in 1851. Although they declined to ordain her, they did in 1859 recommend her as a preacher for life, a "Christian lady of useful gifts as a pulpit speaker," and as "a useful helper in the work of Christ." She eventually became chaplain at the prison in Leavenworth, Kansas, another first for a woman.

In the Free Methodist Church, a large number of women served as licensed "quarterly conference evangelists." They were to be "a class of preachers called of God to preach the Gospel, to labor to promote revivals of religion and spread abroad the cause of Christ in the land," but not in a pastoral charge.

Women preachers were active in other small groups, though neither licensed nor ordained. A group of women preachers existed among the Free Will Baptists (Arminian Baptists) in New Hampshire and Vermont in the late eighteenth century, holding revival meetings all over New England. One also finds references to women preachers among the "Christians," who appear to be a New England offshoot of Congregationalism rather than relatives of the Campbellites. Sarah Righter Major (1808–84), converted in 1826 under the ministry of Whittier's "Pilgrim Stranger," Harriet Livermore, petitioned the Church of the Brethren in 1834 for a license or ordination. They denied her both, but she kept right onr preaching. Of course, Quaker women, particularly those in the revivalist or Hicksite wing like

Lucretia Mott, functioned as preachers though the denomination does not practice ordination.

Women were active in a variety of ministries from the ordained and licensed preaching ministry to local exhorters, class leaders, Bible teachers, and benevolent society "visitors." Many were honored by the publication of autobiographies and biographies, which gave them the opportunity to be role models for other women. Especially fascinating were a group of women like Jennie Smith, "the Railroad Evangelist," who witnessed from their invalid couches. Smith was dramatically healed and continued her writing and speaking ministry. Despite the anticlerical stance of the organized woman suffrage movement, women ministers were always highly honored by these groups and given prominence on platforms, committees, and executive slates. Meetings were often opened and closed with prayers by women clergy.

THE GOSPEL OF REFORM

Revivalism spawned another form of ministry. Some might call it a secularized form, but in the minds of Finneyites it was rather a corollary of evangelism: the reform lecturer. Theodore Weld was probably the archetypal example. After his conversion, Arthur Tappan hired him to lecture on temperance and the desirability of manual training in literary institutions. He became involved in abolition, and within two years converted the majority of the people of the Ohio Valley to immediate abolition. When his own voice failed, he and Henry Stanton trained the Seventy, a group of abolitionist missionary agents that included the Grimké sisters. They in turn became the first woman's rights lecturers, though they were soon joined by many others. Oberlin trained Stone, Brown, Cutler, Cowles, and Sallie Holley. Others, such as Stanton, Anthony, Abby Kelley Foster, and Mary Livermore, came by different routes.

Many, like Willard, secretly nursed a desire or remembered a call to the ministry. In several places she admitted:

> The deepest thought and desire of my life would have been met,
> if my dear old Mother Church had permitted me to be a minister.

The wandering life of an evangelist or a reformer comes nearest to, but cannot fill the ideal which I early cherished, but did not expect ever publicly to confess.

In another source she says, "I was too timid to go without a call, and so it came about that while my unconstrained preference would long ago have led me to the pastorate, I have failed of it."

But, whether minister or reformer, the messages were similar: selfishness, slavery, drunkenness, discrimination against women were all sinful. Those who continued such practices were damned, excluded from the society of the just, forbidden to enter the coming millennium. Those who wished to repent of their sins and be converted should step forward and sign—church membership rolls, temperance pledges, anti-slavery or suffrage petitions. Converts were counted and became among the elect, admitted to the community of fellow believers, and eligible to attend anniversary week meetings each May at Broadway Tabernacle in New York.

As a result, at least in part, of Finney's revivals, women in nineteenth-century America began to fill new roles as pastors, preachers, evangelists, exhorters, and lecturers. Their goal was to win souls, to usher in the millennium, to institute the kingdom of God on earth. Their critics said allowing women to assume these new roles would change the structure of society. They were right.

CHAPTER 8

AIM AT BEING USEFUL

If filled with the Spirit, you will be useful. You cannot help being useful.

—*Charles Grandison Finney*
Lectures on Revivals of Religion

*N*o period has existed since the creation of the world when it was so easy to do good," declared the *Panoplist and Missionary Magazine* in 1814. The nineteenth century was indeed an age of doing good, of extensive and intensive reform. While the Benevolence Empire was largely a creation of the first quarter of the century, Finney's understanding of salvation as a turning from selfishness to benevolence, expressed in the doing of good works, released a dynamic spirit among his converts which transformed benevolence from philanthropy to reform.

Finney believed that every Christian must be "useful," active in going good. He advised converts to

> set out with a determination to *aim at being useful in the highest degree possible.* They should not rest satisfied with merely being useful, or remaining in a situation where they can do *some* good. But if they see an opportunity where they can do more good, they must embrace it, whatever may be the sacrifice to themselves. No matter what it may cost them, no matter what danger or what suffering, no matter what change in their outward circumstances, or habits, or employment it may lead to.

If taken seriously, those are obviously revolutionary words.

The spirit of the Christian is "necessarily that of the reformer," said Finney. "To the reformation of the world they stand committed." In a set of "Letters on Revivals," published in the *Oberlin Evangelist* 1845–46, Finney decried "The Pernicious Attitude of the Church on the Reforms of the Age" (21 January 1846). He asserted that "the great business of the church is to reform the world—to put away every kind of sin. The church of Christ was originally organized to be a body of reformers." Its job was "the universal reformation of the world" and it should be aggressive in its attempts "to reform individuals, communities, and governments, and never rest until . . . every form of iniquity shall be driven from the earth." He vehemently denounced the clergy for "neglecting or refusing to speak out and act promptly and efficiently on these great questions of reform." Such action, said Finney, grieves and quenches the Spirit, making revivals impossible to promote.

In order to promote revivals, Finney declared, "the church must take right ground in regard to politics" and on slavery, moral reform, and temperance. Finney repeatedly labeled slavery a sin: "The fact is that slavery is, preeminently, the *sin of the church.*" Revivals, he said, would also be hindered if there was resistance to temperance reform or reforms regarding "any question involving human rights." In "A Seared Conscience," in the *Oberlin Evangelist* of 28 April 1841 he lists "Abolition of Slavery, Temperance, Moral Reform, Politics, Business Principles, Physiological and Dietetic Reform" as issues the church must confront. As Antoinette Brown said, "Christianity is the heart and soul of them all, and those reforms which seek to elevate mankind and better their condition, cling round our Christianity, and are a part of it. They are like the cluster of grapes, all clinging about the central stem." Although I have not been able to find where Finney actually mentioned woman's rights, it was not difficult for his students at Oberlin and for others to make that application.

Revivalists have often been charged with offering personalistic answers to social questions, claiming that personal conversion alone will solve the world's ills. Finney could not be charged with this fault. While he felt his own personal calling was primarily to convert sinners, he did not believe in Garrisonian nonresistance. He did not eschew the necessity of political action. By 1848 he was saying, "Moral Government is surely a system of moral suasion, but moral suasion includes whatever is designed and adapted to influence the will of a moral agent." While "a great many people mean by moral suasion nothing more than flattery and palaver," for Finney it also included "law, rewards and punishments." In "The Pernicious Attitude of the Church," he rebuked those who "when efforts are made to secure legislation that shall put these abominations away," are "afraid to employ government lest it would be a departure from the system of moral suasion." In his *Systematic Theology,* he even advocates revolution if a government is unresponsive: "When one form of government fails to meet any longer the necessities of the people, it is the duty of the people to revolutionize. In such cases, it is vain to oppose revolution; for in some way the benevolence of God will bring it about."

THE DUTY OF WOMAN

For Finney's converts, benevolence and reform were a matter of duty, not choice. "Holiness, happiness and usefulness are inseparable," declared a column filler in the *Guide to Holiness.* Women felt themselves to be no exception to this rule. As Sarah Grimké proclaimed in her *Letters on the Equality of the Sexes,*

> WHATSOEVER IT IS MORALLY RIGHT FOR A MAN TO DO, IT IS MORALLY RIGHT FOR A WOMAN TO DO; . . . confusion must exist in the moral world, until woman takes her stand on the same platform with man, and feels that she is clothed by her Maker with the *same rights,* and, of course, that upon her devolve the *same duties.*

Speaking somewhat tongue in cheek, Grimké declared that "as woman is charged with all the sin that exists in the world, it is her solemn duty to labor for its extinction." Religious exercises were not enough: "the woman who prays in sincerity for the regeneration of this guilty world, will accompany her prayers by her labors." Women, said Grimké, must regard themselves, "as they really are, FREE AGENTS." She entreated them "to assert your privileges, and to perform your duties as moral beings."

Angelina Grimké felt this compulsion to be useful from the moment of her conversion in a Presbyterian revival. She felt called to some great mission, though she did not recognize the causes to which she was to devote her life until much later. In a series of letters to Sarah in 1836, she wrestled with the need to be useful. On 3 July she wrote: "The door of usefulness in our [Quaker] Society seems as if it was bar'd and double lock'd to me. I feel no openness among Friends; my spirit is oppressed and heavy laden and shut up in prison." Yet the next day she wrote, "The door of usefulness among *others* seems to have been thrown open in a most unexpected and wonderful manner." The following day she mused, "What have we done with the talents committed to us. I sometimes feel frightened to think of how long I was standing idle in the marketplace" (referring to Jesus' parable of the workers in Matt. 20:1-16). The call to become an antislavery lecturer was just becoming clear to her. Within six months she was writing to her friend Jane Smith (20 January 1837):

> How little! how *very little* I supposed, when I used so often to say "I wish I was a man that I might go out to lecture"—that *I* ever would do such a thing—the idea never crossed my mind that *as a woman* such work would possibly be assigned to me, but the Lord is "wonderful in counsel, excellent in working"—making a way for his people where there seems to be *no* way—Dear Jane, I love the work, I count myself greatly favored in being called to it.

She later wrote another correspondent (20 August 1837): "I believe Woman is bound to labor in all Moral Reformations. Because she is a moral, intellectual, and responsible being, standing on the *same* platform of human rights and human responsibilities with man. . . ."

Other women felt the same need to be useful. Lucy Stone, in a July 1853 love letter to Henry Blackwell concerning her lecturing on abolition, wrote: "The privations I have learned to endure, and the isolation, I scarcely regret; while the certainty that I am *living usefully* brings a deep and *abiding* happiness." Abby Price expressed the same conviction in a speech at the first National Woman's Rights Convention: "Human beings cannot attain true dignity or happiness except by true usefulness. This is true of women as of men. It is their duty, privilege, honor, and bliss to be useful. Therefore give them the opportunity and encouragement." The determination to be useful was one of the original resolutions at Seneca Falls, most likely drafted by Elizabeth Cady Stanton:

> *Resolved, therefore,* That, being invested by the Creator with the same capabilities, and the same consciousness of responsibility for their exercise, it is demonstrably the right and duty of woman, equally with man, to promote every righteous cause by every righteous means.

The duty to be useful empowered women to go beyond traditional roles. Phoebe Palmer, one of the more socially conservative women we have been following, expresses this most clearly:

> The Spirit of truth will never lead us into any unscriptural or unintelligible modes of usefulness. It will not lead us to unseemly or untimely utterances, or to any course which will not betoken soundness of mind. But it may lead us to a course which may occasionally be extraordinary.

The call of God often drew these women far beyond woman's sphere as prescribed by society, and gave them courage to answer their opponents. Lydia Sexton was away on a preaching trip when her son Thomas died. When she packed to leave again soon after his funeral, a neighbor said, "Well, if one of my children died when I was away from home I would never forgive myself." To which Sexton replied that certainly if one's trip were merely to visit friends or to pass time, one would have difficulty forgiving oneself, but "if you were working for God, . . . if your motive-force was to promote the glory of God and the salvation of never-dying souls, you would then feel as I do." Thus she could leave her children in God's hands. Sexton went on to comment that her neighbor was a "kind-hearted and noble lady, with all the warm emotions of a mother's love but without the pressing call of the Spirit to the ministry." As for Sexton herself, she thanked God that she "now had light to pursue a different course."

THE BENEVOLENCE EMPIRE

Middle-class women were in a state of transition. In the colonial and revolutionary periods, they were an important part of the community, equally valued with men as workers, skilled craftspersons, small shopkeepers. On the frontier and in a struggling new nation all hands were needed; society was flexible and innovative. The early national period, however, saw a stratification of women's roles, a codification of the cult of true womanhood, and a drastic limitation on the options open to women, at precisely the same time that the industrial revolution and the rise of the business class gave certain women leisure beyond child-rearing and housekeeping. Almost every person mentioned in this study had domestic servants. In fact, Palmer once chided a friend for pridefully doing all her own housework while neglecting her literary gifts and at the same time depriving some poor woman in her neighborhood of employment.

Thus the Benevolence Empire then (as to a certain extent today) was based on the voluntary work and fund raising of middle-class women. Since the cult of true womanhood decreed that religion was part of woman's natural sphere, it was also natural that in the name of religion women should extend their maternal and domestic expertise to those of the community less able to care for themselves. One of the first benevolent societies in America, founded in 1797 by Isabella Graham, was the Society for the Relief of Poor Widows with Small Children. Graham and her daughter Joanna Bethune were also largely responsible for the growth of the Sunday school movement.

Baptist and Congregational women in Boston in 1800 formed a Female Society for Missionary Purposes to raise money and to organize a "concert of prayer" for home missionaries to the Indians and the "heathen" on the churchless frontier. After the founding of the all-male American Board of Commissioners for Foreign Missions in 1810, women supported foreign missionaries. Their first martyr was young Harriet Atwood Newell (1793–1812), who died on Mauritius Island in the Indian Ocean. Their hero was Ann Hasseltine Judson (1789–1826), who evangelized the women of Burma, sustained the mission and her husband, Adoniram, while he was in prison, and died on the field. Stories by and about Adoniram's subsequent wives, Sarah Hall Boardman (1803–45) and Emily Chubbuck (1817–54), fueled the vision of ultimate usefulness and adventure which led many women to aspire to similar service. Women also gave money to help the American Education Society train ministers, the American Home Missionary Society send pastors to frontier churches, the American Bible Society print Scripture, and the American Tract Society pass out pious literature.

Twentieth-century authors Charles Foster, John R. Bodo, Clifford Griffin, and Joseph R. Gusfield all contend that the thrust of the original Benevolence Empire was socially conservative. "Christianity was a social paliative, a soothing unguent for social sores," says Foster. "The Evangelicals wanted no changes in the social machinery; they would grease the gears." Some society names confirm that analysis: the New York Association for the Relief of Respectable, Aged, Indigent Females; the Philadelphia Society for the Encouragement of Faithful Domestics; the Connecticut Society for the Suppression of Vice and the Promotion of Good Morals. While the participants were motivated by genuine Christian concern, their goals were not to eliminate poverty or social inequity but to teach the poor their proper place, train them in domesticity and religion, sober them up, and make them honest, docile domestics or laborers. Isabella Graham said of her own patron and role model of benevolence, Lady Glenarchy of Edinburgh, "She never encouraged idleness or pride, and often remarked that it was better to assist people to do well in the sphere which Providence had assigned them, than to attempt to raise them beyond it." Nurtured by older forms of Calvinism, these women assumed that social classes were part of God's providence.

The early benevolence societies were not only attempts to socially control the poor, but they were also instruments for social control of men over women. Most societies were under the control of the local pastor who opened each meeting with religious exercises and gave the annual lecture to be reprinted with the society's annual report. The clergy often used these occasions to reinforce the cult of true womanhood. As late as the 1860s, a minister admitted to Sarah Platt Haines Doremus (1802–77), founder of the Woman's Union Missionary Society of America for Heathen Lands, the first women's sending agency, that he always went to the meetings of any women's society in his church because one could never be sure for what women might be praying!

Yet most ministers encouraged women to work in benevolence. As Matthew LaRue Perrine declared ever so patronizingly in his 1817 lecture, *Women Have a Work to Do in the House of God:*

> The pious parent, guardian, husband—and especially, the enlightened and feeling minister of the Gospel, . . . must esteem it one of his most noble and happy employments to cheer and animate the female part of the Church in performing their appropriate duties. As they are circumscribed in their means; and as their sense of modesty and subordination is in proportion to their piety, so it is very easy for parents, husbands, or ministers of the Gospel to check them in their attempts to serve their Lord.

Turning to the female members of his audience, he advised:

> While the pious female, therefore, does not aspire after things too great for her, she discovers that there is a wide field opened for the exercise of all her active powers, in which she may do much for the honour of God and the good of men. . . . Knowing that her true dignity and usefulness consist in filling that station marked out for her by the God of nature and grace, she is satisfied in being an *assistant* of man.

For the first quarter of the nineteenth century, the Benevolence Empire was in many ways an extension of the Presbyterian-Congregational Plan of Union. Methodists were so convinced that the Great Eight were under the control of the Presbygationalists that they formed their own societies. The interlocking directorates were full of Presbygational clergy who believed in a clerically dominated social order. They held a Federalist political philosophy which considered society best controlled by the educated, the well-born, and the wealthy. They thought of themselves as moral stewards or trustees of society.

FROM PHILANTHROPY TO REFORM

In the late 1820s, however, the Benevolence Empire, captured by the Finneyite revivalists, began going through some radical changes. To the older philanthropists' ideas of moral ability and accountability, they added immediatism: immediate radical conversion and immediate reformation of the whole world. Not only were people capable of reforming themselves, but they were also capable of reforming the world. As Beecher noted in shock, the Finneyites treated all sinners alike, "without respect to age or station in society." They welcomed the poor and blacks into their churches, women and blacks into their societies. Against the Boston-Yale Presbygational axis was formed the New York Association of Gentlemen and the Third (Free) Presbytery. A battle for control of the Benevolence Empire ensued. As the Tappans' biographer Bertram Wyatt-Brown suggests, the issues were many: lay versus clerical control, Yorker versus Yankee, yeomen versus urban sophisticates, rural pietists versus timid keepers of the Ark. The Tappans teamed up immediately with the Finneyites. They invited Finney to New York City for a short revival in the summer of 1828 and lured him back in 1832 as pastor of Second Free Presbyterian Church. They founded a magazine to publicize both revivals and benevolent enterprises: the *New York Evangelist.*

Finney did not ask converts to submit to the standing moral order but exhorted them to build a new moral order. He did not call people to order but to excitement and zeal, enthusiasm and participation in a new popular movement emerging in both religion and society. He counseled Christians to form societies outside the church if necessary reforms could not find support among "doctors of divinity, ecclesiastical bodies, colleges and seminaries." He declared it a task for women as well as men.

TRAINING IN REFORMATION

The antislavery movement became the first battleground, then moral reform, then temperance. We will discuss those movements in the next three chapters. Nearly every woman eventually involved in the woman's rights movement was active in one or more other reforms, usually as a training ground. They taught Sunday school and regular school. They were involved in antislavery, moral reform, temperance, and peace societies. During the Civil War many of them worked with the Sanitary Commission. All felt the call to be useful. In the Benevolence Empire they found nourishment for what later blossomed in the woman's movement.

First, these women were genuinely concerned about conditions that oppressed their fellow human beings. Finneyite revivalism stressed Christians' duty to help others, to reform society. They were motivated by a faith and a fervor which sustained them in the face of difficulty and oppression. The Grimké sisters, for example, fought for their own rights primarily because they felt so deeply compelled to continue their battle against slavery.

Second, reform work was a permissible way to get out of the house; to invest energies in something other than husband, children, and household; to find meaningful, purposeful work. Not that they were trying to escape family responsibilities, for their devotion to their families is clear, but the Finneyite and holiness emphasis on usefulness and reform taught women that their call to serve God extended far beyond their own doorsteps, whether husbands or fathers liked it or not.

Third, the Benevolence Empire was an invaluable training ground for women. They founded organizations, kept the books, presided at meetings, spoke in public, wrote for journals, engineered petition campaigns, and celebrated substantial victories. The leaders of the women's movement "served apprenticeship in the reforms which flourished in Western New York," as Whitney Cross notes. "Delayed though it was, this later crusade owed a great deal to the Burned-over District's moral reformation."

Fourth, their consciences were honed by exposure to very real injustice and oppression in a nonthreatening way. Initially they were looking at the oppression of those of another race by those of another region, not their own oppression by their closest relatives.

Fifth, they found outlets for their own rage and hostility in attacking the problems of society. We see this clearly in moral reform. It is equally clear in the rhetoric of Sarah Grimké's

Letters on the Equality of the Sexes and the reports of the Boston Female Anti-Slavery Society, as well as many other such reports.

Sixth, the women mastered sophisticated arguments against social, legal, religious, moral, and political injustice. Schooled in the arguments concerning abolition and temperance, they found it easier to develop cogent defenses of woman's rights. Having reinterpreted biblical arguments in these areas, they could change interpretations of their own roles. Having worked for legal and political change for the slave and the sale of alcohol, they knew what it took to change the system.

And finally, the Benevolence Empire provided an arena for confrontation between men and women over issues which were clearly matters of moral consequence and not simply matters of self-interest. In comparison to the confrontations in which many of the same women participated in the male-dominated Benevolence Empire, the confrontations of the early woman's rights conventions were friendly discussions! The women of the Boston Female Anti-Slavery Society had marched through a mob of their rioting townsmen. Angelina Grimké and Abby Kelley had spoken at a Philadelphia abolition meeting with a mob destroying the building around them. Stone and Anthony had eveything from fruit to rocks hurled at them when discussing abolition and temperance. How could mere words hurt as much? Women who had endured such abuse in other causes could no longer be intimidated. They could stand on their own platforms and return verbal attacks with reasoned arguments; they could meet social opposition with political change.

CHAPTER 9

THE BONDS OF SISTERHOOD

If in calling us thus publicly to advocate the cause of the downtrodden slave, God has unexpectedly placed us in the forefront of the battle which is to be waged against the rights and responsibilities of woman, it would ill become us to shrink from such a contest.

—*Sarah Grimké to Amos Phelps*
3 August 1837

lack slavery in America dates back to 1619. By the nineteenth century, it was obviously the most serious moral and political issue in our society, especially for religiously sensitive men and women. In seeking to abolish it, women discovered woman's rights. In the bonds of slavery they recognized their own bondage.

From colonial times religious leaders had spoken out against the practice: Puritan Samuel Sewall in *Selling of Joseph* (1700) and Quaker John Woolman in *Considerations on the Keeping of Negroes* (1754). Baptists made similar protests. Quaker Anthony Benezet in 1776 convinced the Society of Friends to expel slaveholders—Philadelphia Quakers had organized the country's first antislavery society in 1775. John Wesley agreed that "slavery is the sum of all villanies!" and the Christmas Conference of 1784, which organized American Methodism, instituted measures to exclude slaveowners or slave traders from membership. However, in all groups there was a steady accommodation to southern practice.

In 1817 the American Colonization Society was formed to send free Negroes back to Africa and to recompense slaveholders for their loss. Though supported by many influential politicians, many southerners, and a number of clergymen, it was based on black inferiority and the impossibility of the two races living together.

In the 1820s British evangelicals took the lead, calling for the abolition of slavery in the British Empire, particularly the West

Indies. An antislavery society was founded in 1823. By 1825 it had abandoned gradualism and colonization in favor of immediate abolition, as outlined by Elizabeth Cottman Heyrick in her 1824 pamphlet entitled *Immediate, Not Gradual Abolition.* After serving three months with Finney's Holy Band, Charles Stuart, friend and mentor of Theodore Weld, went to England to aid in the effort. It was he who formulated the "Bible argument" against slavery and in turn convinced Americans, through Weld, to adopt immediate emancipation as their goal.

William Lloyd Garrison was editing a Baptist temperance journal when in 1829 he was converted to the antislavery cause by Quaker Benjamin Lundy. After being jailed for libel and being bailed out by Arthur Tappan, Garrison founded his own journal, the *Liberator,* which began publication 1 January 1831. Within the year Garrison had rallied Boston abolitionists, including Methodist Orange Scott, into the New England Anti-Slavery Society. In 1832 he published his *Thoughts on African Colonization,* denouncing the American Colonization Society and calling for immediate abolition.

In New York, the Finneyites' *Evangelist* was also urging Americans to join the British example and demand immediate abolition. In 1833 when England did indeed ban slavery in the West Indies, Finney, Weld, the Tappan brothers, and others formed the Friends of Immediate Abolition, which in turn organized the New York Anti-Slavery Society amid a riot on 2 October in Chatham Street Chapel. Their publication was the *Emancipator.* By December the New York and Boston groups joined forces in Philadelphia to form the American Anti-Slavery Society with Arthur Tappan as president. By 1837 the society had 145 local chapters in Massachusetts, 274 in New York, and 213 in Ohio.

THE LANE REBELS

Immediate abolition, however, was not a popular idea at first. In February 1834 the issue came up for debate at Lane Seminary in Cincinnati, to which the Tappans had contributed, of which Beecher was president, and at which Weld had been quietly proselytizing for abolition for several months. For nine nights the students considered the question, Ought the people of the slaveholding states to abolish slavery immediately? At first Beecher consented to participate, but after counsel with advisors he even declined to attend, sending his daughters Catharine and Harriet instead. It was essentially a revival: a protracted meeting which opened and closed each session with prayer, attended by private daily prayer meetings. After listening to southern students and freed slaves testify to the cruelties of slavery, and to Weld and Henry Stanton expound the moral issues, the students voted unanimously for immediate abolition. For another nine evenings they then discussed whether or not the American Colonization Society's goals were such as to "entitle it to the patronage of the Christian community." The answer was negative, despite Catharine Beecher's presentation of her father's plan of assimilation, which would somehow have found a canopy broad enough to encompass both colonizationists and abolitionists.

Many of the trustees were upset; Beecher was equivocal; and eventually the students were expelled. They, trustee Asa Mahan, and the Tappans' money transferred to Oberlin. Nineteen of the "Lane Rebels" later joined the Seventy. Beecher called them "the offspring of the Oneida denunciatory revivals," but Stanton said, "I had fears that there might be some unpleasant excitement, particularly as slaveholders and prospective heirs to slave property were to participate in it. But the kindest feelings prevailed. There was no . . . denunciation." In fact, he said, they studied the issues as those "whose polar star was fact and truth, whose needle was conscience, whose chart was the Bible."

Interestingly, the debate was replayed three years later when Catharine Beecher published *An Essay on Slavery and Abolitionism, with Reference to the Duty of American Females*. Angelina Grimké replied with *Letters to Catherine [sic] E. Beecher, in Reply to An Essay on Slavery and Abolitionism*. Beecher argued that it was unfeminine and unchristian for women to join abolition societies, sign petitions, or even concern themselves with such issues of national policy. Angelina replied that women had every right—and responsibility—to think, speak, and act on all the great moral questions of the day. Woman's right to do so could not be given or taken away by men because *"her rights are an integral part of her* moral being," created by and responsible to God alone.

In 1835 many of the Lane Rebels took up residence at Oberlin. Weld abolitionized the Western Reserve, Pennsylvania, and upstate New York, while Stanton did the same in Rhode Island and Connecticut. Mahan, as president of Oberlin, was a committed abolitionist, as was Professor Finney, who notes in his *Memoirs:*

> When I first went to New York, I had made up my mind on the question of slavery, and was exceedingly anxious to arouse public attention to the subject. I did not, however, turn aside to make it a hobby, or divert the attention of the people from the work of converting souls. Nevertheless, in my prayers and preaching, I so often alluded to slavery, and denounced it, that a considerable excitement came to exist among the people.

At Oberlin he spoke on behalf of abolition at various gatherings, wrote of it in the *Oberlin Evangelist,* was active in the Ohio Anti-Slavery Society as vice-president in 1835 and 1839, and attended anniversary conventions of the American Anti-Slavery Society, often held in his New York churches. He helped formulate the movement's "higher law" arguments as a basis for disobedience to the Fugitive Slave Law.

Finney, however, was a bit more conservative than some of his friends. The Tappans favored social integration, *amalgamation* as it was then termed, including completely free seating in Broadway Tabernacle. Though Finney felt that was going too far, vandals set fire to the construction, and firemen refused to put the fire out on the basis of the rumors. Certainly the Lane Rebels both preached and practiced full integration, though it was not practiced fully at Oberlin. Finney himself was committed to preaching the whole gospel, salvation and reform. He counseled Weld in 1836 to "make abolition an appendage" of revivals because he felt that if "the publick mind can be engrossed with the subject of salvation" slavery could be eliminated in two years! On the other hand, in a letter to Weld in 1837, he expressed the fear that "we are in our present course going fast into a civil war. . . . Have you no fear of this? If not, why have you not?" He felt that Weld and Stanton were "good men" but not always "wise men," and sometimes reckless. He predicted abolitionist denunciation "in a censorious spirit" could result in "the church and world, ecclesiastical and state leaders [becoming] embroiled in one common infernal squabble that will roll a wave of blood over the land."

Indeed, riots were becoming common. In Boston, members of the Female Anti-Slavery Society planned to hear British abolitionist George Thompson speak on 21 October 1835. Twenty-five members managed to enter their upper meeting room, but a hundred more were turned back by a mob. Garrison addressed the meeting briefly and then left, only to be caught by the mob and led through the streets. The women, holding hands for support, marched bravely from the building to the home of a member and completed their meeting there. The same night in Utica, New York, six hundred delegates to the New York State Anti-Slavery Society meeting were disturbed by rioters.

A feeling was growing that all hands were needed if abolition was to succeed in the face of growing hostility. As Augustus Wattles, one of the Lane Rebels, wrote Betsey Mix Cowles (9 April 1836):

> "In Christ Jesus there is neither male nor female." That is, in moral enterprises, moral worth and intellect are the standard. A mind whether deposited in a male or female body is equally valuable for all moral and intellectual purposes. Indeed there is no station in life but what may be filled as ably and as beneficially by woman as by man. The difference is made principally by education. Abolition is opening a new field for female effort. I pray you sieze [*sic*] with avidity the opportunity thus offered to redeem your character and name from unjust reproach.

THE SEVENTY

By late 1836, Weld's body was exhausted and his voice permanently impaired by his devotion to the cause, so he retired to New York City to become an agent for the American Anti-Slavery Society. In October and November, he and Stanton held intensive training sessions—following many of Finney's new measures techniques—for the Seventy, which included the Grimké sisters, Orange Scott, and nineteen of the Lane Rebels. Many of them had previously worked as missionary agents for tract, temperance, and Bible societies. This time abolition was their mission. The Grimkés were included because of their associations with Garrison and Weld, but the agency committee of the American Anti-Slavery Society had already voted in the summer of 1836 to hire women agents. Weld indoctrinated them in the abolitionist creed that slaveholding was a sin because it gave human beings a power over others that is reserved for God. The remedy for this sin as for others was repentance and conversion.

The Grimké sisters were sent north to New England under the auspices of the American Anti-Slavery Society and the newly formed Female Anti-Slavery Society. Their crowds soon became too large for parlors, and they moved into churches— primarily Methodist, Baptist, and Unitarian because Congregationalists and Quakers had both voted to ban antislavery lectures from their buildings. Curious about what the women were saying, men began to sneak into their meetings in late June. Said Sarah, "One brother wanted to come and another thought he had a right and now the door is wide open. Whoever will come and hear our testimony may come." Weld initially replied, "God give thee a mouth and wisdom to prophesy like the daughters of Philip, like Huldah and Deborah."

However, their activities brought down the wrath of the Congregational clergy already wary of abolitionism, which was being promoted more vigorously by Methodists and Baptists. They met in the North Brookfield, Massachussetts, Congregational Church. Lucy Stone watched from the balcony: "I was young enough then so my indignation blazed . . . and I told my cousin that, if ever I had anything to say in public, I should say it, and all the more because of that Pastoral Letter." The pastors clearly saw the Grimké sisters as a threat to their station. They mourned the loss of "deference to the pastoral office" and protested lectures "within parochial limits of settled pastors without their consent"—the same complaint lodged against Finney's Holy Band. Said the *Letter,* "Deference and subordination are essential to the happiness of society, and peculiarly so in the relation of a people to their pastor." They also saw the Grimkés as a threat to "female character."

According to their reading of the New Testament, women were to be "unobtrusive and quiet," always "conscious of that weakness which God has given her for her protection." Gilson, in her notes for a biography of Brown, summarized the situation:

> The New England Association shuddered, beset by their doubts about Biblical authority for freeing the slave, their certainties about the intentions of God and St. Paul in regard to women, and their deeply felt but half unconscious belief that their own hitherto impregnable position of power was being assailed, they produced the "Pastoral Letter."

RIGHTS TO DEFEND

Thus was born the woman's rights movement. The Grimké sisters knew intuitively, despite Weld's advice to claim their Quakerism and proceed as though nothing had changed, that they must defend not only their own rights but also every woman's right to speak and act. Wrote Angelina to her friend Jane Smith (10 August 1837): "the rights of the slave and woman blend like the colors of the rainbow." Sarah reminded Weld (20 August 1837) that

> *this invasion of our rights* was just such an attack upon *us,* as that made upon Abolitionists generally when they were told a few years ago that *they had no right* to discuss the subject of Slavery. Did *you* take no notice of this assertion? Why no! With one heart and one voice you said, *We* will settle *this right before* we go one step further. . . .
>
> . . . If then we "give *no reason for the hope that is in us,"* that *we have equal rights* with our brethren, how can we expect to be permitted *much longer to exercise those rights?* . . . if we are to do any good in the Anti Slavery cause, our *right* to labor in it *must* be firmly established. . . . *we* cannot push Abolitionism forward with all our might *until* we take up the stumbling block out of the road.

So Sarah wrote a series of "Letters on the Province of Woman" for the *New England Spectator,* which were collected as *Letters on the Equality of the Sexes and the Condition of Women.* They received support from the Finneyites. Henry

Stanton shared their platform and introduced their lectures with a "precious prayer." Mary Mahan wrote to ask if Angelina would come to assist Alice Cowles in the Female Department at Oberlin and if she could not do that, could she at least write something for the Young Ladies Anti-Slavery Society. The Grimkés continued to speak for six months, holding at least eighty-eight meetings in sixty-seven towns, speaking to at least forty thousand people. On 21 February 1838 Angelina addressed the Massachusetts State Legislature, the first woman to do so.

Angelina and Theodore Weld were married 14 May 1838 in Philadelphia. Because so many churches were closed to them, Philadelphia reformers decided to build their own Pennsylvania Hall to be dedicated that same day. Angelina was to speak two days later. As she rose to speak, the building was surrounded by a noisy mob, and bricks came crashing through the new windows. She gave her finest speech, describing for more than an hour the horrors of slavery as she had experienced it. She was followed by a brief speech from Abby Kelley (Foster) (1810–87), who had been inspired by hearing the sisters in Massachusetts. Weld was so impressed with her abilities that he urged her to become an antislavery lecturer herself: "Abby, if you don't, God will smite you!" The next day Lucretia Mott presided over a meeting. The mob was so unruly that the mayor warned the women to leave—which they finally did, arm in arm, black and white together—further infuriating the mob. That night the building was burned to the ground.

ANTISLAVERY DIVISIONS

The issue of women's role in the movement was a controversial one, even for abolitionists. The crisis came in 1840, when Abby Kelley was nominated to the business committee of the American Anti-Slavery Society. Lewis Tappan and friends walked out and formed the American and Foreign Anti-Slavery Society. Some have tried to blame the split entirely on the woman issue, implying that the Finneyites opposed women's participation while the more radical and liberal Boston crowd welcomed it. Of course the issues were much more complex.

Tensions had always existed between the uncompromising Garrison and the New York crowd. Ever more radical, Garrison was deeply anticlerical, antigovernment, basically anarchistic. His extremism alienated Boston colleagues like Orange Scott, who wrote the New Yorkers in 1839 saying, "There *must be* a new organization in this state [Massachusetts], and I believe we are about ripe for it. I think I can pledge *9/10ths* of the Methodist influence in the State for a new State society." Many abolitionists in New York and Ohio, such as James G. Birney, Myron Holley (Sallie's father), and Stanton, felt that political action was the next step since the petition campaign had been gagged. They formed the Liberty Party, which did admit women, and ran Birney in the 1840 presidential campaign. The movement was also feeling the fallout of the 1837 financial depression and acrimonious split in the Presbyterian church, which was a blow to all Presbygational reform activity. The split can be regarded as the first North-South division, since the Old School was stronger in the South and the New School more numerous in areas of the North where revivalist abolitionism reigned. The church itself did not officially split over slavery until 1861, a division which was overcome only in 1983.

American divisions were exported when Garrison's group sent Lucretia Mott (1783–1880) as a delegate to the London World's Anti-Slavery Convention in late 1840. Following the lead of Weld and Grimké, Stanton and Cady were wed. The trip was their honeymoon. For Elizabeth, meeting Mott and seeing the women excluded from the convention was consciousness raising. As the women talked in the balcony, they vowed to organize for woman's rights upon their return to America. It took them eight years.

CHURCH DIVISIONS

Abolition was strong among Methodists, rooted in John Wesley's antipathy to slavery and encouraged by their British cousins' example. By 1838, six of sixteen northern conferences had antislavery majorities, and three others had very vocal abolitionist minorities. Of three thousand ministers, seven hundred elders were willing to preach and vote against slavery, as were that many more local or lay preachers. The greatest increase in membership was taking place in the most strongly antislavery conferences. Probably as many as fifty thousand members were abolitionist. A Methodist Anti-Slavery Society had been formed in 1834. Many of the abolitionists were also holiness advocates. Slavery, however, was also strong. By 1843, twelve hundred Methodist clergy owned about 1,500 slaves and laypeople owned another 208,000 slaves. Growing southern defense of slavery—publications offering scriptural defenses, conference resolutions denying that it was sinful—alienated even moderate northern leaders who thought all Christians agreed slavery to be sinful, but who had tolerated it as a matter of political and economic expediency. And then there were the black Methodists. By 1844, 13 percent of all Methodists were black, about 145,000, and one-third of all southern black Christians were Methodist.

At the General Conference of 1836, the Methodists declared slavery to be evil but also condemned "modern abolitionism." The 1840 conference again silenced the radical abolitionists, which led to defection of the Wesleyan Methodist Church in Michigan in 1841 and the Methodist Wesleyan Connection in New York in 1842 and 1843. In 1844 they became the Wesleyan Methodist Connection, led by such ardent abolitionists as Orange Scott, La Roy Sunderland, and Luther Lee. Debate in 1844 over a slaveholding bishop made it clear the Methodist Episcopal church must divide North and South.

At the same time, Baptists were similarly dividing into the Northern and Southern Baptist churches over the issue. Other churches were agitated by the issues but did not divide—either because they were not held together by any national organization to divide, or they were regional in their strength.

During the 1840s the Finneyite abolitionists were trying a more political tack, supporting the Liberty Party. Weld and the Grimkés settled in Fort Lee, New Jersey, and he worked in the New York office of the American and Foreign Anti-Slavery Society. In 1839 the sisters had shared their own memories and clipped vivid illustrations from various papers to help Weld write *American Slavery As It Is*. The book gave many shocking stories of women's degradation, including one of a master's rape of a Methodist slave. In 1841, Weld went to Washington,

D.C., leaving the sisters to cope with their growing family and farm while he researched, wrote, and lobbied for abolition on behalf of a group of Whig legislators—all of whom were Christians—five Presbyterian elders, and several "revival men," including three who were Weld's own converts.

WOMAN'S RIGHTS

One of the first speeches devoted to woman's rights, other than at Oberlin, was given by Lucy Stone in 1847 at her brother Bowman's church in Gardner, Massachusetts. Her father came to listen, but at first buried his head in his hands in shame. As he listened, he gradually straightened up. By the end of her speech, he was sitting tall and proud. The next spring she visited Abby Kelley Foster's home, and Abby wrote the Massachusetts Anti-Slavery Society asking why they were not using Stone as a lecturer. Samuel May, their general agent, immediately hired her. Eventually she too felt the same pressures the Grimkés had felt. She responded: "I was a woman before I was an abolitionist. I must speak for the women." In 1851 the West Brookfield church expelled her. After a two-year courtship, Stone married Henry Blackwell on 1 May 1855, but she insisted on keeping her own name and in pursuing her own goals.

In 1848, after starting their family in Boston, the Stantons moved to Seneca Falls in upstate New York. When Elizabeth heard that Mott was visiting nearby, she renewed their acquaintance. The result was the long-delayed woman's rights meeting, held 19–20 July 1848 in the Wesleyan Methodist Chapel in Seneca Falls. They drafted a Declaration of Principles, modeled on the Declaration of Independence, and followed it with a series of resolutions. Despite only one brief newspaper notice of the meeting, three hundred people came from a fifty-mile radius. The woman's rights movement was launched.

News of the event spread quickly to Ohio. On 19 April 1850 a woman's rights convention was held in the Second Baptist Church at Salem with Betsey Mix Cowles as president. It was the first meeting at which men were totally denied a voice. "Never did men so suffer!" comments the *History of Woman Suffrage*. At the closing banquet men were allowed to purchase tickets which entitled them to sit in a balcony, smell the food, and hear the speeches.

In 1851 the women of Ohio held a convention in Akron in May and at Mount Gilead in December. In May 1852 they organized the Ohio Woman's Rights Association in Massillon, with Hannah Tracy as president. In May 1853 they met in Ravenna. Caroline Seymour Severance presided, and Antoinette Brown spoke. In October the fourth annual National Woman's Rights Convention was held in Cleveland with Mahan, Brown, Stone, Severance, and other Oberlin women in attendance.

The third National Woman's Rights Convention had been held in Syracuse in September 1852. Paulina Kellogg Wright Davis chaired the convening committee. Antoinette Brown spoke eloquently on the Bible. One of the most sympathetic local supporters was Luther Lee. An ardent abolitionist, he had been the Wesleyan Methodist's first president in 1844 and for eight years editor of *The True Wesleyan.*

In September 1853 the antislavery society held a meeting on a Sunday morning in New York City, and that night Antoinette Brown preached to fifty thousand people. During that same week the women met in convention at Finney's Tabernacle. In November 1853 another convention was held in Rochester. Amelia Jenks Bloomer (1818–95) and Brown were among the meeting's vice-presidents; Anthony was secretary. While Finney was holding meetings during the winter of 1854–55 in Western and Rome, the women met in nearby Albany. This time Stanton was president, Brown on the business committee, and Anthony secretary. In the fall of 1856, the seventh National Woman's Rights Convention met in Finney's Broadway Tabernacle.

The women continued to meet until the beginning of the Civil War, holding a convention in Albany in February 1861. During the war they did not meet in convention but did form the National Woman's Loyal League in New York in May 1863. Angelina Grimké came out of retirement to raise her voice at the meeting. They pledged to support the Union and to collect a million signatures on petitions asking Congress to pass the Thirteenth Amendment. They also worked in the Sanitary Commission, bringing aid to the troops.

As the war drew to a close, the debates over support for the Fourteenth and Fifteenth amendments splintered the movement. In 1866 the National Woman's Rights Association officially changed its name to the American Equal Rights Association, hoping to combine with the American Anti-Slavery Society. They appealed to Congress for universal suffrage and equal rights. But it was becoming clear by 1868 that women were not going to be included, so Anthony formed the Woman Suffrage Association. After all their work, Stanton and Anthony particularly were outraged that all women should be asked to take a step back as black men were given a step forward. They were increasingly at odds with another faction of the movement, led by Stone and Livermore, which was willing to put the resolution of abolition first. The break came in 1869. In May the Equal Rights Association held its last meeting. At its conclusion, without informing their rivals, Stanton and Anthony founded the National Woman Suffrage Association (NWSA). Feeling betrayed by Stanton's and Anthony's outright lies and double-dealing, Stone, Livermore, Henry Blackwell, along with such Finneyites as Brown, Severance, Cutler, Abby Kelley, and Methodists Amanda Way and Gilbert Haven, formed the American Woman Suffrage Association (AWSA). For twenty years the movement was divided and increasingly ineffective.

Thus the first impetus to woman's rights was abolition. In *The Slavery of Sex: Feminist-Abolitionists in America*, Blanche Glassman Hersh argues that most significant was the strength of their religious beliefs: "Though they rejected the orthodox tenets and formal trappings of Protestantism, their personal perfectionism and sense of moral duty and 'calling' sustained them through difficult trials." As deeply religious people, "they felt that divine will placed them in a position to fight for the emancipation of women as well as of slaves, and they responded to what they considered a sacred obligation."

CHAPTER 10

FEMALES WHO HAVE DEVIATED FROM THE PATHS OF VIRTUE

The great object of Moral Reform is to shut out . . .
the men *who are licentious, and oblige them to have*
not society. . . . The work of exclusion is done for
the women; let Moral Reform do it for the men.
—Advocate of Moral Reform (1835)

*W*omen's work for the abolition of slavery raised the issue of woman's rights. Moral reform raised their feminist consciousness.

In the spring of 1830, shortly after Charles Finney's first New York City revival, a young Princeton divinity student, John R. McDowall, arrived in the big city to work as a summer missionary for the American Tract Society. With women converts from Finney's crusade, he held Sunday school classes in prisons and almshouses in the notorious Five Points area. The region, north of Chatham Street, south of Canal, and west of the Bowery, had become a swamp for the poor, the desperate, the derelict. City residents viewed it as "a great moral ulcer located in the very heart of the city; being only a few hundred yards from the City Hall and Park, and within three minutes' walk, and in plain view of Broadway" which bordered it to the west. The Old Brewery had been erected there in 1792 as a factory, but in 1837 it had been converted into a dwelling—a warren—housing hundreds of souls, several families to a room, Irish, blacks, and later Italians. Said Charles Dickens after a visit there in 1842, it was characterized by "poverty, wretchedness, and vice, . . . reeking everywhere with dirt and filth," housing "all that is loathsome, drooping, and decayed."

John McDowall, in his youthful idealism, also became concerned about the prostitutes of the area. Arthur Tappan, who had visited the Magdalen Asylum in London, wanted to duplicate the British efforts. So with McDowall as superintendent, he and the Association of Gentlemen founded the Magdalen Society of New York and persuaded it to open the Asylum for Females Who Have Deviated from the Paths of Virtue.

McDowall, dedicated to his work, had the instincts of a social worker. Within a year he had collected the facts and published them graphically in *The Magdalen Report,* which he had persuaded Tappan and two physicians to endorse. All were unprepared for the shock and outrage which greeted their report. First, city fathers at Tammany Hall were chagrined at McDowall's statistics claiming that "every tenth female in our city is a prostitute," ten thousand in all, with a working-life expectancy of only five years. Second, they were infuriated that instead of blaming prostitution on the moral weakness of women, McDowall pointed his finger at the men of wealth and status who patronized them.

Tappan stood by McDowall when he was tried by the presbytery on charges of being an irresponsible scandal-monger and an obscene seeker of notoriety, but he quietly closed the Magdalen "house of refuge." Yet McDowall would not back down. In 1832 he enlarged his charges in a second report, *Magdalen Facts,* and he began publication of the monthly *McDowall's Journal.* The breach between McDowall and the Association of Gentlemen became increasingly bitter, with charges of financial irresponsibility being traded.

Tappan formed a successor, the Society for Promoting the Observance of the Seventh Commandment. He declared it would have no asylums:

> An asylum . . . is not the Gospel mode of converting sinners. Did Jesus Christ say "Go ye into all the world and build *asylums* for every sinner?" Never! . . . The word of God is "the sword of the spirit," and if properly wielded by Christians would subjugate more sinners . . . in three months than all the asylums on earth would ever rescue from damnation.

He had given up on the reform of prostitutes, but he would still denounce prostitution by preaching morality.

MORAL REFORM

The Finneyite women were not so easily discouraged. On 12 May 1834 they rallied to form the Female Moral Reform Society. Lydia Andrews Finney was elected first directress. Finney addressed the society at a December 1834 meeting in Chatham Chapel and encouraged their work. He told them to "visit these houses, and fill them with Bibles and Tracts and make them places of religious conversations and of prayer, and convert their wretched inmates *on the spot."*

In the final issue of *McDowall's Journal,* 28 January 1835, McDowall published the full text of the accusations made against him and his own point-by-point rebuttal. And then, in what might be called a journalistic will entitled "To My Friends," he made a final bequest:

> To the New York Female Moral Reform Society, I give the *Journal* and all the donations placed at my disposal to promote the cause. . . .
>
> These ladies defended my character through evil report, and through good report. They stood by me in dark hours, when sorrows of oppression weighed heavily on my soul, and brought my partner nigh unto death.

The women retitled the *Journal* the *Advocate of Moral Reform.* By 1837 they had sixteen thousand subscribers, the majority of them in the burned-over district. Lucy Stone's family subscribed to it along with the *Liberator,* the *Anti-Slavery Standard,* and the *Oberlin Evangelist.* It was also standard reading matter in the Brown home. The Grimké sisters wrote for it. Sophia Clarke sent a monetary contribution.

The first goal of its publishers and editors was to convert the nation to moral purity; converting and reforming the lost women of the city was a secondary concern. They attacked the problem at its source by publishing the initials and hometowns of men known to frequent the brothels! Following Finney's advice, they collected the information by talking with the brothel's inmates and by standing on the streets in front of notorious houses, taking down information.

Exhibiting an unspoken feminism in their institutional

history, by 1836 the Moral Reform Society had hired two women to edit the *Advocate* and two other women as agents to tour New England and New York State, explaining the work, organizing auxiliaries, soliciting subscriptions. By 1839 the society had 445 branches and had become a national organization, the American Female Moral Reform Society. The next year there were 555 local chapters. The "house of refuge" which Tappan had abandoned was changed from a place for the conversion of prostitutes to an employment agency for women because the society realized that most women became prostitutes out of economic need, not moral depravity. It also hired two female missionaries. In 1841 it hired a woman bookkeeper; in 1843, women typesetters and assemblers. Eventually the organization was staffed entirely by women, a very unusual phenomenon for the age.

The women of the executive committee of the New York society constituted themselves as visitors and began canvassing assigned districts. By 1837 they were spending so much time visiting that they voted to pay themselves salaries. At first they visited middle- and lower-class homes, fearful of the rich and the poor, but by 1838 they began reaching out tentatively to the poor and finally concentrated their efforts there, seeking to get at the root causes behind prostitution. After the financial Panic of 1837 multiplied urban problems, the women became experts concerning slum conditions. They were actually doing very much the same kind of thing Jane Addams became famous for pulling together at Hull House half a century later.

In 1847 they founded the Home for the Friendless and the House of Industry, giving shelter to indigent women, offering education, an employment agency, job training, piecework, sewing machine rental, union organizing, an industrial school for children, family counseling. They published in-depth analyses of public health conditions, housing, milk inspection, and prisons. They forced the city to hire female wardens for female prisoners, and they lobbied for an antiseduction law in 1848 to curb "white slavery." In the 1850s they increasingly defined reform in environmental terms and began to work more directly with children. In 1848 they were renamed the American Female Guardian Society and Home for the Friendless.

The movement spread, particularly in areas where the Finneyites were strong. For example, in 1834 in Utica, revivalist pastor Samuel Aiken of First Presbyterian Church had preached on "Moral Reform." Viewing Utica's increasing urbanization, he warned that "a whole tribe of libertines" was about to invade the city. He charged the women, "Daughters of America! Why not marshall yourselves in bands and become a terror to evildoers!" Paulina Wright Davis played a leading role in the founding of the Utica Moral Reform Society in 1837 with 100 members. Actually Utica women were slow—nearby Whitesboro had begun a chapter in 1835 with 40 members; by 1837 the Clinton society had 84, and the Westmoreland branch had 181. McDowall had visited Whitestown in 1835 and uncovered "alarming statistics" of lewdness and obscenity. In 1841 the Utica group formed a visiting committee which visited the poor, gathering information on sexual offenses and domestic crimes against women. That same year they gathered nearly three thousand signatures on petitions to outlaw prostitution. They marched on city hall to demand statistics on sex offenders. They interrogated bartenders about frequent customers, and they accosted men of dubious character on the streets. They even took to court the case of a young servant who reported sexual exploitation by her employer. They provided legal counsel and a better job. Members of the society were frequent correspondents and financial contributors to the *Advocate of Moral Reform.*

All women students at Oberlin were urged to become members of the local Moral Reform Society. In the 1840s Lucy Stone was its secretary-treasurer and one of its leading spirits. Antoinette Brown served on its executive committee. Male students had their own Moral Reform Society—the cause seemed particularly to attract male seminarians in a number of schools.

FIVE POINTS MISSION

An allied effort was the Five Points House of Industry, founded in 1854, mainly through the efforts of members of the Ladies' Home Missionary Society of the Methodist Episcopal Church, which had been formed in 1844 by members of the New

York Female Missionary Society. Phoebe Palmer was a prime mover in this effort. Their initial motivation was the conversion of the poor. Members had been visiting the poor and the sick, holding Bible classes, Sunday schools, and prayer meetings in the Five Points area since 1843.

They wanted to provide a permanent chapel and a resident minister, so in May 1850 they hired Louis M. Pease. Together they saw the causes of poverty as intemperance and unemployment. Gradually, however, they came to see drunkenness not as a lack of moral fortitude to be remedied by signing pledges and reading tracts, but as a response to the want and despair of slum life. Pease immediately arranged with a local textile manufacturer to get piecework, and converted his evening prayer meeting room into a sewing shop by day. Within a week he had forty women working. By February 1851 Pease had gotten sixty adults regular employment as a result of the training they had received, and forty-two were presently learning sewing, baking, cobbling. Eventually the Five Points Mission purchased the Old Brewery, demolished the building, and built a new structure to provide a chapel, schoolroom, baths, and twenty rent-free apartments.

Like the Female Moral Reform Society, the women of the Five Points Mission also began to concentrate on saving the children from street gangs, educating them, offering day care and even adoption. Commented an attorney on their efforts, "What no legal enactment could accomplish—what no machinery of municipal government could effect, . . . women have brought about, quietly but thoroughly and triumphantly."

Like the Moral Reform Society, the Five Points Mission also became a training ground for women. It was here that Maggie Newton Van Cott began her preaching career. It was also to the Five Points Mission that Antoinette Brown came upon her graduation from Oberlin. Reported Brown:

> Mrs. Palmer, the Methodist exhorter, who was doing such efficient work in her own denomination and in philanthropy, took me to a meeting in which we both took part, then drove me back to my boarding-place in her carriage, showing extreme marks of kindness and friendliness.

Although Brown did not work long at the mission because she felt her strong woman's rights views were unacceptable, she did share the women's vision of urban reform. After a period of traveling and lecturing on temperance, abolition, and woman's rights, she spent 1855 in New York City, working in the slums. She wrote about her experiences for Horace Greeley's *New York Tribune,* and the articles became a book, *Shadows of Our Social System* (1856). On 24 January of that same year she married Lucy Stone's brother-in-law, Samuel Blackwell. Although the bearing of seven children left her little time for the public platform, she did do three hours of "habitual brain work" every day, producing a number of books.

Typical of the women's efforts was the work of Sarah Platt Haines Doremus (1802–77). A Presbyterian who joined her husband's Dutch Reformed church, she began holding Sunday services in the city prison in the 1830s. Along with Abby Hopper Gibbons (1801–93), she became a leader of the Women's Prison Association, incorporated in 1854, serving as first director in 1867. She devoted much time to the association's Home for Discharged Female Convicts, later name the Isaac T. Hopper Home, an enterprise for rehabilitation. In 1850 she was also one of the founders of the New York House and School of Industry, which provided work for poor women and schooling for their children. She became its president in 1867. In 1854 she helped found the Nursery and Child's Hospital, which provided day and hospital care for poor children. She helped found the Presbyterian Home for Aged Women, served on boards of the City Mission and Tract Society and the City Bible Society, and made possible the opening in 1855 of the Woman's Hospital. She is usually noted only as founder of the Woman's Union Missionary Society, the first independent society to send and support women as missionaries.

SISTERHOOD

Because moral reform, and concern for the poor, the sick, and the imprisoned were initially less controversial reforms than abolition, a broader, more conservative spectrum of women were drawn to them. Secure in the feeling that they were participating in a more socially acceptable form of Christian social service, they let down their guard, they became deeply involved, and in the end they became more radicalized. A truly feminist consciousness was raised.

They began with a natural sympathy which became empathy and sisterhood. Said the ladies of the Women's Prison Association, "Woman is the natural . . . aid of woman in her needs; the woman that feels this not has yet to learn her mission aright." They continued: "Among the most precious of woman's rights, is the right to do good to her own sex. . . . Every woman in misfortune or disgrace is the proper object of care to the happier and safer part of her sex."

Angelina Grimké declared, "I am sure that the poor and oppressed . . . can never be benefitted without mingling with them on terms of equality." And thus the New York Moral Reform Society noted in the 1843 *Advocate:* "In seeking to promote . . . the elevation of our own sex . . . we recognize no distinctions of station, or clime or color." They expressed their solidarity with the "poor squaw" and the "slave woman" whom they called "our sisters in bonds." Women at the Hopper Home were not to be treated by volunteers "with a supercilious, a cold, a spurious kindness, but as a *woman* and a *sister.*" Doremus urged "every woman . . . to aid in healing her suffering sisters."

Barbara J. Berg, in her book *The Remembered Gate: Origins of American Feminism, the Woman and the City, 1800–1860,* argues that "woman's sense of the oppression of her sex originated in American cities. It matured slowly as upper- and middle-class women began to assimilate the meaning of their intense involvement both with one another and with the destitute of their sex." This involvement brought into focus not only the oppression of the poor, but its similarities with their own oppression. And in the name of others they could give it a name.

The *Guide to Holiness* was an outlet for women's religious testimonies; the *Advocate of Moral Reform* was an outlet for religious women's hostilities. Typical were titles such as "Licentious Males More to Be Despised than Licentious Females." Letters from rural readers detailed the seduction of innocent girls by certain men who yet retained their good name

in society. Most letters described specific incidents, but many
simply voiced anger. Commenting on the double standard and
men's attitudes to the seduced woman, one reader declared in
1834:

> Honorable men, they would not plunder; a mean action they
> despise; an imputation on *their honour* might cost a man his life's
> blood. And yet they are so passingly mean, so utterly
> contemptible, as basely and treacherously to contrive . . . the
> destruction of happiness, peace, morality, and all that is
> endearing in social life; they plunge into degradation, misery,
> and ruin those whom they profess to love. O let them not be
> trusted.

The editors wrote in the same tone (1835): "It makes us
indignant that our sex should any longer be imposed upon by
men, who pass as gentlemen and yet are guilty of loathsome and
disgusting conduct. It is a justice which we owe to each other, to
expose their names." In 1838 the *Advocate* printed a pledge
which women could sign saying that they would socially shun
profligate men.

Speaking of prostitution, the Female Benevolent Society
described the "deep-laid schemes of treachery against female
innocence." A treatise on the New York Police Department
had suggested that "the vast number of loose women that infest
the streets of the city . . . are . . . so totally bereft of shame, that
they are . . . beyond the possibility of reform." In reply the
Benevolent Society declared: "It cannot be concealed that the
treachery of man, betraying the interests of . . . woman, is one
of the principal causes, which furnishes the victims of
licentiousness. Few, very few . . . have sought their wretched
calling." They too urged society "to brand the seducer with the
infamy that he deserves." They suggested that "every virtuous
female utterly refuse to associate with [profligate men], let her
feel herself to be polluted by their presence, let them be
regarded as enemies to the sex."

Nor was criticism of men confined to lechers. The *Advocate*
for 15 February 1838 noted:

> A portion of the inhabitants of this favored land are groaning
> under a despotism, which seems to be modeled precisely after

that of the Autocrat of Russia. . . . We allude to the tyranny exercised in the HOME department, where lordly man, "clothed with a little brief authority," rules his trembling subjects with a rod of iron, conscious of entire impunity, and exalting in his fancied superiority. . . .

Instead of regarding his wife as a help-mate for him, an equal sharer in his joys and sorrows, he looks upon her as a useful article of furniture, which is valuable only for the benefit derived from it, but which may be thrown aside at pleasure.

They saw this situation not just among the "vicious poor" but also among Christians, even leading ones, members of the Moral Reform Society, and even in ministers' families. Finney's praying women were again trying to begin reformation at home.

Their ire was directed not only at men but also at the religious establishment. When ministerial support was not forthcoming, the *Advocate* in 1835 asked, "How long shall Christian women wait the movement of their pastors in the great work of Moral Reform? . . . And how long shall we wait for their approval?" Again in 1837 the editors asked, "Where are our religious papers on this subject? Are they not all like dumb dogs that *dare* not bark?"

A SENSE OF AUTONOMY

Working for the elevation of their own sex, women found their own power, a sense of authority, and autonomy. The *Advocate,* delineating "The Province of Woman" in 1837 declared:

We have been reproached in the cant language of infidelity for leaving the kitchen and nursery to meddle in matters that concerned us not. . . .Why . . . should we be stigmatized as amazons, who have committed an unprecedented breach of decorum, when we appear as advocates of the cause of moral reform?

They went on to say:

We wish our sex to feel that they have a personal responsibility in *all* that concerns the . . . good of society, and that they can no more transfer this responsibility to their fathers, husbands, sons,

or brothers than they can relinquish their own personal
identity. . . . [Women] are capable . . . of thinking for
themselves, judging for themselves, and acting for themselves.

Commenting on a series of feminist lectures in New York in
1858, the *Advocate*'s editors agreed that the "principle which
many of the advocates of women's rights contend for is simply
this . . . that a woman is always in her sphere when she is doing
what God has given her that faculty to do."

The editors noted that there is "no feeling more universal
among . . . human beings than the desire to be independent, to
take care of themselves." They urged mothers to educate their
daughters to "far greater self-reliance," advocating that "no
woman of health and sound mind should allow herself to feel
dependent on any body." They printed a comment by a woman
from Wheaton, Illinois, who looked forward to the day "when
woman comes to occupy her true position . . . and is allowed to
qualify herself for self-support."

A writer in the *Advocate* in 1845 urged that daughters "be
taught to look forward to marriage with rational hopes and
expectations." Let them, she said, "be made to feel that love
and marriage are not essential to their respectability, usefulness
and comfort." In 1858 the *Advocate*'s editors suggested that

> every girl should have a trade, a business, a profession, or some
> honorable and useful way of gaining a livelihood—some
> employment in which her powers of body and mind may be
> amply developed. If she has not, she will be dependent upon
> somebody, and her dependence will degrade her.

Analyzing the economic basis for much of women's
oppression, the editors protested the unequal pay between men
and women. "A Plea for Female Operatives" in the 1846 *Ladies
Wreath* criticized "those calling themselves gentlemen" who
prefer "a garment made by a woman because she will do it for
half price, and it will be quite as well done."

Eventually, like the abolitionists, they concluded that
political action was the answer. Said a writer in the *Advocate*
(1838): "Our deep and strong impression of opinion should be
heard through the *ballot box* on this subject to which our
lawmakers should be compelled to listen, to which their action

should be made to respond." They undertook a petition drive to get seduction and adultery punished as crimes. The *Advocate* invited women of Boston, Philadelphia, Albany, Troy, Utica, Rochester, and Buffalo to join the crusade. In 1840 the New York Moral Reform Society sent twenty thousand petitions to the state legislature; Ohio chapters did almost equally well.

After the Civil War the cause was taken up by the WCTU as a Committee for Work with Fallen Women, formed in 1877, for the conversion of prostitutes. In 1883 it became the Department for the Suppression of the Social Evil; in 1885, the Department of Social Purity, the White Shield-White Cross program. Part of their program in the 1890s was to raise the age of consent. In 1886 the age of consent in twenty states was ten. One state put it at seven! By 1894 all but four states in the South had raised it above ten; twenty had set it at sixteen.

Male-identified historians have tended to see the negative sides of these programs, their sometimes apparently negative views of sexuality. Within their own context, however, these women were trying, before the age of contraception, to gain control over their own bodies, to put an end to the double standard, and to combat sexual abuse and domestic violence. As the editor of the *Advocate* asked in 1835, "Has God made a distinction in regard to the two sexes in this respect? Is it any where said that what is sin in one, is not sin in the other?" Said the third annual report of the Boston Female Moral Reform Society in 1838: "in maintaining the *rights* of women, we will not neglect her appropriate duties, one of the principal of which duties is to guard our daughters, sisters, and female acquaintances from the delusive arts of corrupt and unprincipled men." As Lucy Stone wrote to Antoinette Brown in 1855, "The right to vote will yet be swallowed up in the real question, viz.: has woman a right to herself? It is very little to me to have the right to vote, to own property, etc., if I may not keep my body, and its uses, in my absolute right."

Carroll Smith Rosenberg, in her study of *Religion and the Rise of the American City: The New York City Mission Movement 1812–1870,* summarizes the movement:

> With such close ties to Finney and his new theology—and the commitment it implied to Christian action—the ladies of the

Moral Reform Society occupied an extreme wing in the evangelical movement. They were not content to remain at home, satisfied with educating their children in the ways of piety and with praying for the millennium. Finney's preaching had convinced them that silence in the face of sin amounted to complicity. Like the New York abolitionists—many, of course, Finneyites, . . .—they felt themselves unable any longer to compromise with the devil; sin must be assailed wherever and in whatever form it existed.

Within their religious context, however, the members of the Female Moral Reform societies were not extremists—those were the preachers, the abolitionists, the woman's rights lecturers. These were ordinary middle-class wives and mothers fighting for their homes, their families, their less-fortunate sisters, *their* homes, *their* families. In the process they found feminism.

CHAPTER 11

TO TOUCH IT WAS CONTAMINATION

*It had been with many, a fearful struggle to yield up
their preconceived ideas of what was a lady's place,
and what the world might think and say. Not a few
carried the subject to their closets, and there on their
knees fought the battle with self and pride before the
Lord, till He gave them strength and they came forth
anointed for the war.*

—Mother Eliza Daniel Stewart

*O*ne of the ironies of history is that abolitionists, despised by the majority of their contemporaries, have been lauded by historians, while temperance advocates, almost uniformly respected in their day, have been dismissed as meddlers, cranks, neurotics. In Oneida County, New York, neither abolitionists nor moral reformers were invited to march in the Fourth of July parades, but temperance societies were. While the Woman's Christian Temperance Union, the WCTU, was the largest and most respected women's group of its day, its members' grandchildren often view it with scorn. Yet alcoholism and drug addiction, the evils it sought to combat, are still among our nation's greatest health problems.

In the colonial period alcohol consumption was moderate and accepted, regulated within the tightly knit family and community setting. Apprentices often shared a pint with their master or mistress during lunch or around the fire in the evening. In the late eighteenth century only a few Quakers and the Methodists raised their voices against hard liquor. In 1784 their objections were underlined by Dr. Benjamin Rush's *Inquiry into the Effects of Ardent Spirits on the Mind and Body.* The Methodist General Conference imposed strict limitations on the use of distilled liquor in 1790 but did not urge total abstinence until 1832.

The first temperance organization appears to be the Union Temperance Society, founded in 1808 by a William Clark of

Saratoga County, New York. In 1813 the Massachusetts Society for the Suppression of Intemperance and the Connecticut Society for the Reformation of Morals were founded.

After Lyman Beecher gave and published a series of six sermons against alcohol, the American Temperance Society was founded in February 1826 (its official name was the American Society for the Promotion of Temperance). Its pledge was not just moderation but abstinence from hard liquor. Its first national convention was held in 1833. In 1836 it was renamed the American Temperance Union, and its pledge was made teetotal. The organization became moribund after the Panic of 1837. Many of the Finneyites, including Finney himself, supported temperance and also had a strong interest in the Graham diet (essentially vegetarian with an emphasis on whole grains and water), manual labor, homeopathic medicine, and other health matters. Oberlin was a manual labor school and observed a Graham diet.

In April 1840 the Washingtonian movement was born in Baltimore when a group of drinkers, sitting around a bar, vowed to go on the wagon. They did, and many others followed their example. Its auxiliary was called the Martha Washington Society. During the 1840s other organizations, such as the Sons and Daughters of Temperance, peaked in membership. Another active group was the Order of Good Templars, which eventually accepted women as equal members after the Civil War. Generally in the 1850s the question of slavery claimed national attention, but temperance remained a major force in state and local politics, achieving remarkable, if temporary, gains. It was in 1851 that Maine passed a law prohibiting the manufacture and sale of intoxicating beverages within the state. Within four years thirteen states had similar laws. By 1855 all of New England, New York State, and large parts of the Midwest were dry, but by the war such laws had virtually disappeared.

WOMEN REBUFFED

In 1852 the New York Temperance Society, an all-male organization, issued a call for "Temperance associations of every name . . . to send delegates" to a June convention in

Syracuse. The newly formed Woman's State Temperance Society sent Susan B. Anthony and Amelia Jenks Bloomer. Their rights were defended by Luther Lee, local Wesleyan Methodist pastor, but they were denied admission after a vicious, daylong debate.

That night Lee welcomed the women into his church to hold their own meeting, which drew a packed house. Lee, Anthony, and Samuel J. May spoke. Bloomer reported it in the July issue of her paper, the *Lily*.

A similar incident happened the following year when Antoinette Brown and Caroline Severance tested the waters at the Whole World's Temperance Convention. Delegates were debating whether or not to seat women. Brown and Severance were at a woman's rights convention nearby and decided, along with Wendell Phillips, to walk over and see if they would be admitted. Brown had credentials anyway as a delegate from both the Rochester and South Butler temperance societies.

When they arrived, Brown quietly walked up to the secretary and handed him her credentials. He told her that he could not rule on their validity himself, but that there was currently a motion on the floor to receive all delegates without distinction of color or sex. So she sat down. The resolution passed, and she went to the platform "for the purpose of thanking them for their course, and merely to express my sympathy with the cause and their present movement." She intended then to go back to the woman's rights meeting. Her request to speak occasioned a long debate. Eventually she was duly recognized but still had to stand on the platform for three hours while men raised all sorts of parliamentary objections.

During her trial, she said later, "friends" crowded around her and tried to get her to leave peaceably, but she stood her ground. One asked if she thought that Christ would have made such a scene, and suddenly, she said, "there came rushing over my soul the words of Christ: 'I came not to send peace, but a sword.' It seems almost to be spoken with an audible voice, and it sways the spirit more than all things else." She stood firm in a peace and strength of spirit she felt was from God. "There were angry men confronting me, and I caught the flashing of defiant eyes," she recalled later, "but above me, and within me, and all around me, there was a spirit stronger than they all. At that moment not the combined powers of earth and hell could have tempted me to do otherwise than to stand firm."

The affair moved Horace Greeley to report: *"First day*—Crowding a woman off the platform. *Second day*—Gagging her. *Third day*—Voting that she shall stay gagged. Having thus disposed of the main question, we presume the incidentals will be finished this morning."

The *History of Woman Suffrage,* after reporting this incident, comments:

> Most of the liberal men and women now withdrew from all temperance organizations, leaving the movement in the hands of time-serving priests and politicians, who, being in the majority, effectually blocked the progress of the reform for the time—destroying, as they did, the enthusiasm of the women in trying to press it as a moral principle, and the hope of the men, who intended to carry it as a political measure.

Other analyses suggest that the country was otherwise preoccupied with the war.

THE CRUSADE

The temperance movement came to life again dramatically in the Crusade of 1873–74 led by two Ohio women. Eliza Daniel Stewart (1816–1908), a devout Methodist, lived in Athens, Ohio, where she organized a lodge of Good Templars in 1858 and gave her first temperance lecture at a Band of Hope meeting. During the Civil War, she worked with the Sanitary Commission, gathering supplies and visiting camps in the South, earning the name "Mother Stewart." In 1866 the Stewarts moved to Springfield, Ohio, and it was there the next year that she organized the city's first woman suffrage organization and became its president. On 22 January 1872 her "temperance warfare" began in earnest when she gave a lecture seeking to get women to prosecute drunkards under Ohio's Adair Act, which was passed in 1854 and amended in 1870, giving wives and mothers of alcoholics the right to sue liquor dealers for damages if they sold alcohol to these men. She herself aided women in taking several cases to court, even addressing the jury. After her second victory in October 1873, the women of Springfield petitioned the city council for a local option ordinance banning liquor. At nearby Osborn, Mother Stewart organized the first Woman's Temperance League in 1873.

Simultaneously in Hillsboro, Ohio, Eliza Jane Trimble Thompson (1821–99), another devout Methodist woman, was being aroused on the same issue. Diocletian Lewis had come to town to lecture. On 22 December 1873 he had given his talk on "Our Girls." An advocate of homeopathic medicine and physical exercise for women, he had been concerned about the temperance issue ever since his father "had forgotten everything but drink," leaving his mother with five children to raise. Because of the abuse, she would sometimes cry in her children's presence. But in the 1830s she also had the fortitude to persuade the women of Clarkesville, New York, to confront liquor dealers and get them to promise to stop selling alcohol. The Hillsboro audience asked Lewis to give his free temperance lecture, "The Duty of Christian Women in the Cause of Temperance," on Sunday, 23 December. He had given the same lecture for years in many places, but this time was different.

Eliza Thompson did not attend, but her children did. They came home and told her she should get involved. Her father, a prominent Presbyterian and Ohio politician, had been the first president of the Ohio Temperance Society and in 1836 had taken her to a national convention in Saratoga, New York, where she was the only woman. Her oldest son, Allen, a promising young minister, was being destroyed by alcoholism. Thus, after prayer, she went to a meeting the next day at the Presbyterian church and was elected president of the group. She led them forth to make a personal appeal to liquor-selling druggists. Next they visited a saloon where Thompson knelt on the floor and led them in prayer. Such visits continued steadily for the next three months until their activities were stopped by court injunction.

Similar groups of women were mobilized in Fredonia, New York, and Washington Court House, Ohio. As news of their activities spread, other communities launched similar crusades.

Ohio saw activities in 130 other towns; Michigan had 36 cities affected, Indiana 34, Pennsylvania 26, and New Jersey 17. By the end, the Crusade had taken root in 912 communities in 31 states and territories. Nationwide 750 breweries closed, and production of malt liquor dropped by 5.5 million gallons. About 32,000 women in Ohio and nearly 60,000 nationwide participated.

The next August a number of Methodist women gathered at Lake Chautauqua, New York, for a Sunday school teachers' institute. There, as the women talked of the Crusade, they formed a committee and called a national meeting for Cleveland in November. It began 18 November 1874 in the Second Presbyterian Church with sixteen states represented, 135 registered women delegates and another 175 visitors. Methodist preacher and organizer of the Woman's Foreign Missionary Society, Jennie Fowler Willing (1834–1916), chaired the opening session. That same summer Frances Willard had gone east to Boston to meet Dio Lewis and to New York City to talk with women active in temperance there. She also visited the Gospel Temperance Camp Meeting at Old Orchard Beach, Maine, a holiness campground. One evening she gave a speech before three thousand people, and it was well received. In Cleveland, Annie Wittenmyer, founder of the Methodist Home Missionary Society and editor of the *Christian Woman,* who had done distinguished work with the Sanitary Commission, was elected president of the newly formed Woman's Christian Temperance Union. Willard was elected corresponding secretary. She plunged into the work—writing letters, speaking, organizing, traveling.

Then Willard was converted to the suffrage cause. She was well aware of the movement, of Anthony's and Stanton's National Woman Suffrage Association and Stone's and Livermore's American Woman Suffrage Association. But the latter was weak and the former was deeply mired in such unsavory issues as George Francis Train's politics, Victoria Woodhull's "free love" views of marriage and divorce, and Henry Ward Beecher's alleged adultery. Thus to raise the suffrage issue in the WCTU was quite controversial. As she said later:

Be assured, dear friends, it has not been a pleasant duty thus to act or speak as we women of the West have felt called upon to do. But, for one, let me tell you, that on my knees one Sunday morning in the room of a veteran crusader in Columbus, Ohio, it came to me, as I believe, from God, that I was to speak and act for this cause. I knew it meant criticism; it meant alienation, perhaps, of confidence and influence, but I acted according to my conscience, and my light. . . .

When she finally spoke out on the issue at the WCTU's convention in Newark in 1876, she began her speech with an anecdote about a black man who, in the act of saving the lives of three white men during the Civil War, had shouted, "Somebody's got to be killed, and it might as well be me." She noted later that some of her good friends wept at the story "at the thought of ostracism which, from that day to this, has been its sequel—not as a rule, but a painful exception." She closed by saying that friends had urged her to "fight behind masked batteries a little longer," and "so I have been fighting hitherto; but it is a style of warfare altogether foreign to my temperament and mode of life." Instead she decided to join the cavalry forces "in this great spiritual war," where trumpets and bugles call "strong souls onward to a victory which Heaven might envy, and 'Where, behind the dim Unknown,/Standeth God within the shadow,/Keeping watch above His own.' "

When she finished, a woman described as having held aloof from the suffragists because of fears for their orthodoxy—quite possibly Hannah Whitall Smith—now felt duty-bound to join the cause, and so she said:

I asked God to gather up my prejudices as a bundle and lay them aside. They remained tangible and tough, but I laid them aside. . . . It came after nights of waking and weeping, for I felt the dear Lord was preparing me for something, and He did not want me to be burdened with that bundle. Now, in Methodist parlance, "my way grows brighter and brighter."

The story is told by Ray (Rachel) Strachey, Smith's granddaughter, an ardent feminist who marched with her grandmother in British suffrage demonstrations.

Although it took several years, Willard became president of

the WCTU in 1879 and proceeded to make it not only a temperance but also a suffrage organization. Although no southern states were represented at the convention which elected her, and conservatives argued that a favorable vote on suffrage would close the South to temperance work, in 1881 Willard toured and thoroughly organized the South, forging the first successful postwar cooperative effort between North and South. In 1883 she organized the West. In 1880 she secured endorsement of her home protection ballot; by 1882 a franchise department was in operation; and in 1883 the WCTU endorsed an equal suffrage plank without a vote in opposition.

SUFFRAGE TRAINING GROUND

On the national level, and particularly on the state level, there is a remarkable overlap in leadership between the temperance and the suffrage movements. Most often women were initially active in temperance, gaining there a training in organization and a confidence in their leadership abilities, and then they became active in suffrage. Anna Howard Shaw, for example, was superintendent of the WCTU's Department of Franchise from 1888 to 1892 before becoming vice-president of NAWSA under Susan B. Anthony from 1892 to 1904 and president in her own right from 1904 to 1915.

On the state level a number of women stand out. Methodist laywoman Caroline Elizabeth Thomas Merrick (1825–1908) made arrangements in 1882 for Willard to speak in New Orleans. From 1883 to 1893, Merrick headed the Louisiana WCTU and from 1896 to 1900 the state suffrage association. Similarly in Mississippi, Belle Kearney (1863–1939), converted in a Methodist revival, experienced her calling when she first heard Willard speak in 1889. In 1891 she became a national lecturer and organizer for the WCTU and served as president of the Mississippi chapter in 1895. She called the organization "the liberator of Southern women." From 1906 to 1908 she was president of the Mississippi Woman Suffrage Association, which grew directly out of the WCTU. In 1924 she became the state's first woman state senator.

In Indiana the movements were also closely tied. Quaker Amanda Way (1828–1914), who became a Methodist preacher, called the state's first woman's rights convention at an 1851 abolition meeting. She became first vice-president of the Indiana Woman's Rights Society. In 1854 she organized the Woman's Temperance Army; she also was active in the Order of Good Templars, being the first female Grand Worthy Chief Templar. In 1869 she reactivated woman's rights by organizing the Indiana Woman Suffrage Association, affiliated with Stone's AWSA. Active in the Crusade of the 1870s, she then moved to Kansas where in 1880 she became founder and first president of that state's WCTU.

Surrounding Way were a group of strong leaders. Zerelda Gray Sanders Wallace (1817–1901), a member of the Christian Church (Campbellite), was one of the delegates to the Cleveland founding convention of the WCTU. She helped organize the Indiana WCTU, serving as president from 1874 to 1877 and from 1879 to 1883. From 1883 to 1888, she was national superintendent of the franchise department. In 1878 she also helped organize the Indianapolis Equal Suffrage Society, affiliated with Stone's AWSA. Another friend and colleague was Methodist Dr. Mary Frame Myers Thomas (1816–88). Initially active in the Order of Good Templars, she edited the *Lily* after Amelia Bloomer. In 1856 she became president of the Indiana Woman's Rights Society. She helped reactivate the Indiana Woman Suffrage Association in 1869. She was to serve also as state superintendent of franchise for the WCTU. Another associate in the 1880s was Presbyterian lawyer Helen Mar Jackson Gougar (1843–1907). Presbyterian Mary Garrett Hay (1857–1928) was treasurer of the Indiana WCTU for seven years and by 1885 superintendent of a national department. She joined a local suffrage association in 1895, working closely with Carrie Chapman Catt. After moving to New York, she was president of the New York Equal Suffrage League from 1910 to 1918 and the New York City Woman Suffrage Party from 1912 to 1918.

Mary Rice Livermore, a lifelong friend and colleague of Willard, was active before the war in the Washingtonian temperance movement and during the war in the Sanitary Commission. In 1868 she became founder and president of the Illinois Woman Suffrage Association. Another colleague was Catharine Van Valkenburg Waite (1829–1913), an 1853

Oberlin graduate, who was elected president of the Illinois association in 1871. Livermore subsequently moved to Massachusetts to serve for a time as editor of Stone's *Woman's Journal.* She was a founder of both the Massachusetts WCTU and the state's Woman Suffrage Association, serving as president of the former from 1875 to 1885 and of the latter from 1893 to 1903. Jennie Fowler Willing was the first editor of *Our Union* and served several terms as president of the Illinois WCTU.

In Ohio, Harriet Taylor Upton (1853–1945) began as secretary of a local county chapter of the WCTU in Warren and eventually served for eighteen years as president of the Ohio Woman Suffrage Association.

In Michigan, abolitionist Quaker Laura Smith Haviland (1808–98), who served as a minister of the Wesleyan Methodist Church from 1844 to 1872 and who founded the Raisin Institute to educate blacks "on the Oberlin plan," worked for temperance and suffrage in her later years. She concludes the fourth edition of her autobiography, *A Woman's Life Work* (1887), with the cry "the saloon must go!" She continued to work for suffrage in Kansas when she was in her eighties.

Ada Matilda Cole Bittenbender (1848–1925), Presbyterian lawyer, organized the Nebraska Woman Suffrage Association in 1881, serving as president in 1882. The same year she became active in the Nebraska WCTU, serving from 1883 to 1889 as state superintendent of temperance legislation. From 1887 to 1892 she was superintendent of legislation and petitions for the national WCTU.

In Arkansas, devout Methodist Minnie Ursula Oliver Scott Rutherford Fuller (1868–1946), who also studied law, was active in the state WCTU before serving from 1907 to 1917 as national superintendent of the Department of Juvenile Courts, Industrial Education and Anti–Child Labor Efforts. In 1911 she helped found the Political Equality League in Little Rock and served in 1914 as first vice-president of the Arkansas Woman Suffrage Association.

For Willard, the WCTU and the NAWSA were sisters. She commented in an 1891 address:

Our friends have said that, as President of the National American Woman Suffrage Association, Mrs. Stanton leads the largest army of women outside, and I the largest one inside, the realm of conservative theology. However this may be, I rejoice to see the day when, . . . I can clasp hands in loyal comradeship.

THE HOME PROTECTION BALLOT

How did Frances Willard convince vast numbers of ordinary, churchgoing middle-class women that they wanted to vote when the suffrage movement by and large had only alienated them?

Biographer Mary Earhart offers several reasons for Willard's success. First, "her astute analysis of human nature and public opinion created one of many differences between her and older leaders. Mrs. Stanton based her futile arguments on reason, Miss Willard based her appeal on emotion." Second,

the vast majority of women were interested in just two things—their homes and their church. Of all the women-leaders of that period, she alone had the imagination to see that any reform movement which would enlist the women must be associated with these two special institutions.

Willard motivated the women of the WCTU by putting arguments about the woman question on a different plane. She made suffrage work a matter of selfless service, a matter of Christian duty, rather than one of selfish rights. As Willard noted in her *Home Protection Manual,* a handbook of strategy:

During past years the brave women who pioneered the equal suffrage movement, and whose perceptions of justice were keen as a Damascus blade, took for their rallying cry: "Taxation without representation is tyranny." But the average woman, who has nothing to be taxed, declines to go forth to battle on that issue. Since the Crusade, plain, practical temperance people have begun appealing to this same average woman, saying, "With your vote we can close the saloons that tempt your boys to ruin" and behold! they have transfixed with the arrow of conviction that mother's heart, and she is ready for the fray. Not rights, but duties; not her need alone, but that of her children and her country; not the "woman," but the "human" question is stirring women's hearts and breaking down their prejudice to-day.

In her 1876 speech she quotes a granddaughter of Jonathan Edwards, "a woman with no toleration toward the Suffrage movement," who nevertheless declared, "If, with the ballot in our hands, we can, as I firmly believe, put down this awful traffic, I am ready to lead the women of my town to the polls, as I have often led them to the rum shops."

Second, Willard grounded her emotional appeals in the highly charged rhetoric of what historian Barbara Welter has called "the cult of true womanhood," or, to use Nancy Cott's phrase, "the cult of domesticity." Welter has demonstrated that in the nineteenth century, woman's sphere was marked by piety, purity, submissiveness, and domesticity. Willard's watchwords were *mother* and *home,* usually capitalized. She assumed that women were innately religious, "familiar with the pages of the Book of God, busied with sacred duties of the home and gracious deeds of charity." She also assumed that women were pure. She argued that women could be counted on to vote wisely on all issues because "we are fortunate in belonging to the less tainted half of the race"! Women also have another instinct, "much higher and more sacred" which "reaches up toward Heaven—the instinct of a mother's love, a wife's devotion, a sister's faithfulness, a daughter's loyalty!" In fact, "mother-love works magic for humanity, but organized mother-love works miracles. Mother-hearted women are called to be the saviors of the race." According to Willard, "What the world most needs is mothering."

Woman's natural sphere was, of course, the home: "Home is woman's climate, her vital breath, her native air. A true woman carries home with her everywhere. . . . for the home is but the efflorescence of woman's nature under the nurture of Christ's gospel." Accepting the rhetoric, Willard did, however, expand the sphere a bit: she defined the WCTU's purpose as "to make the whole world homelike." Women should "come into government and purify it. . . . for woman will make homelike every place she enters, and she will enter every place on this round earth!"

Willard was not, however, an advocate of woman's submission, despite her use of the rhetoric of true womanhood. In the home she envisioned, husband and wife practiced the

"Christian method of two-fold headship," the "Christian method of dual headship."

AN APPEAL TO THE CHURCHES

Finally, Willard made her appeal pointedly palatable to churchwomen. Drawing on that stream of revived and consecrated churchwomen energized by Charles Finney's revivalism and the holiness preached by Finney, Palmer, and Whitall Smith, she channeled their gifts into her do-everything policy. She assessed her own organization's work astutely:

> Perhaps the most significant outcome of this movement was the knowledge of their own power gained by the conservative women of the churches. They had never even seen a "woman's rights convention," and had been held aloof from the "suffragists" by fears as to their orthodoxy; but now there were women prominent in all church cares and duties eager to clasp hands for a more aggressive work than such women had ever before dreamed of undertaking.

Finney had declared that "in earth's affairs God works by means"; Willard's genius was in articulating those "means" and convincing conservative, home-loving churchwomen to carry them out.

Local and national temperance meetings were usually held in churches. Religious exercises such as prayer, Bible readings, and hymns were always a vital part of WCTU meetings. Ministers, men and women, were prominent in all proceedings. For example, when the WCTU held its 1880 convention in Boston, delegates were welcomed to the city by the Rev. A. J. Gordon, leading holiness advocate, pastor of Park Street Church, and founder of what is now Gordon College and Gordon-Conwell Theological Seminary. Maria Gordon, who had been a strong supporter of Willard's work with Moody, gave morning devotions. During the world's WCTU convention there in 1891, women filled the pulpits of sixty Boston churches. Ministers were asked to endorse the women's efforts to secure the ballot—a suggested form letter soliciting a minister's support was even supplied in the *Home Protection Manual*.

Willard appealed to churchwomen because she was herself a committed Christian and churchwoman. Raised in a devoutly Christian family, she had been converted and baptized as a young adult. She had experienced holiness, and she had served the church's institutions.

A VISION OF EQUALITY

Yet while she used the rhetoric of domesticity, separate spheres, home, and motherhood, Willard also articulated an egalitarian vision more deeply rooted in the evangelical tradition of Finney and Palmer. Woman is, she said, "first of all a daughter of God, whose powers of thought and action should be left free that she may know the truth; and that next she is a daughter of humanity, whose relation to the state should be equal to that of her brother, man."

Biographer Lydia Trowbridge says Willard was also responsible for the Temperance Declaration of Principles, which reads in part: "We believe that God created both man and woman in His own image, and therefore we believe in one standard of purity for both men and women, and in the equal right of all to hold opinions, and to express the same with equal freedom."

After the Fall, Willard admitted, men and women "began to drift apart, he into the realm of force and she into that of seclusion," but ideally in Christ's kingdom, "man and woman have been steadily traveling back to Eden." She synthesized the two strands of domesticity and egalitarianism in her 1887 presidential address:

> Under the curse, man has mapped out the state as his largest sphere, and the home as woman's largest; under the blessing, man and woman shall map out home as the one true state, and she who, during centuries of training, has learned how to govern there, shall help man make the great, cold, heartless state a warm, kind and protecting home. The White Ribbon women are tired of this unnatural two worlds in one, where men and women dwell apart; they would invade the solitude of the masculine intellect; break in upon the stereotyped routine of the masculine hierarchy in church and state; and ring out in clear but gentle voices the oft-repeated declaration of the Master whom they serve: "Behold, I make all things new."

As a result of her egalitarian reading of the Bible, she concluded that "whatsoever in custom or law is contrary to that love of one's neighbor which would give me or her all the rights and privileges that one's self enjoys, is but a relic of brute force, and is to be cast out as evil." As she told the first International Council of Women, headed by Susan B. Anthony, at its meeting in Washington, D.C., in 1888:

> God made woman with all her faculties, her traits, her way of looking at all great questions from the highest to the lowest, and he made her to be a helpmeet for man, and he made man to be a helpmeet for her; he made them to stand side by side, sun-crowned; he made them stand in a republic, as I believe, bearing equally its magnificent burdens.

Above all, Willard was herself a master organizer. She called it her do-everything policy. Said one man in eulogizing her, before Willard,

> reformers had nearly all been "one idea" people, who treated some one particular reform as a panacea, exaggerating its importance and failing to appreciate its need of cooperating moral forces. With her great heart she saw that all reforms were but fragments of one reform, the Christianizing of society.

CHAPTER 12

MUTUAL SUBMISSION, ACTIVE DISCIPLESHIP

We acknowledge that we have encouraged men to prideful domination and women to irresponsible passivity. So we call both men and women to mutual submission and active discipleship.

—*Chicago Declaration, 1973*
Evangelicals for Social Action

*W*hen the Nineteenth Amendment granting women the right to vote passed the House of Representatives on 10 January 1918, women in the gallery broke into the doxology, "Praise God from Whom All Blessings Flow."

They would have to wait until 4 June 1919 for the Senate to pass the measure and then until 26 August 1920 for enough states to ratify its adoption. Of the early leaders, only Antoinette Brown Blackwell lived to cast her vote in the presidential election that year. An era had come to an end, and another had begun.

Women had won the right to vote, but most of the other issues for which they struggled remained to be won—equality under the law for all women regardless of race or class, property rights, equal pay, divorce, the right to their own bodies, rights to their children, equal opportunity in careers, full equality in church or synagogue. Some have argued that the movement died after suffrage was won. Others suggest that it simply broadened out. Margaret Sanger (1879–1966) continued to lead the crusade to make contraception available to all. Women ventured into higher education and a variety of careers. Some even tested the waters of elective and appointive politics.

Having survived World War I, Americans had to cope with the growing failure of Prohibition, the Great Depression, World War II, and Korea. By the 1950s the ideal of the middle-class home served by a nurturing wife and mother became a national symbol for normalcy.

Reaction set in with the publication of Simone de Beauvoir's *Second Sex* (English, 1953) and Betty Friedan's *Feminine Mystique* (1963). The women's movement was reborn in the 1960s, again side by side with black civil rights.

Politically women focused on the Equal Rights Amendment, first introduced in 1923, seeking to guarantee that "equality of rights under the law shall not be denied or abridged by the United States or any State on account of sex." The ERA finally passed the House of Representatives on 15 August 1970 and the Senate on 22 March 1972, but it failed to win ratification by two-thirds of the states. It was reintroduced in Congress in 1983. Women have received some equity through the 1964 Civil Rights Act, the Equal Pay Act, and state equal rights amendments.

THE DECLINE AND RESURRECTION OF EVANGELICALISM

The evangelical revivalism and reform which Finney's revivals spawned dissipated after the Civil War. Several factors were involved. First, the Protestant majority declined in the face of increased immigration by Roman Catholics and Jews. The Evangelical United Front simply no longer represented consensus. America had become a pluralistic nation.

Second, the onslaught of scholarship—biblical criticism, historicism, evolution, social Darwinism, socialism, Marxism—fragmented Christendom. Much of evangelicalism adopted Old School, Princeton theology formulations which are antithetical to Finneyite revivalism. A large segment of the church became fundamentalist, more concerned with theological, intellectual questions than with ethical, social issues; more concerned with preserving the faith than Christianizing society.

Third, as Ernest Sandeen argues in *The Roots of Fundamentalism*, the optimistic belief that Christians could usher in the millennial kingdom of God on earth (postmillennialism) gave way to pessimistic convictions that Christians were living in history's last dispensation before Christ's second coming, that the world was getting worse and worse no matter what good people might do, that true Christians would soon be rescued from this evil world by the Rapture (premillennialism). Concocted by British theologian John Nelson Darby in the

1830s, it infected most of American evangelicalism by 1900, siphoning off almost all impulse to social reform.

Dispensationalists were more impressed with sin than with redemption, more convinced of the world's sinfulness than God's love and power. Any attempt to ameliorate society was futile and only postponed Christ's coming. One could only rescue individuals through inner-city "rescue missions" for the poor and alcoholic, and the Florence Crittenden homes for unwed mothers. The fundamentalist-modernist controversy in the 1910s and 1920s split the Presbyterian Church, U.S.A., and the American Baptists. It still troubles the Southern Baptists.

In the main-line denominations women's struggles shifted from ordination to laity rights—the rights of laypeople, men and particularly women—to gain voting privileges. Frances Willard had been a pioneer in the Methodist church. She was followed by such women as Belle Harris Bennett (1852–1922). In the Episcopal church, Laura Clay helped lead the fight. In many conservative denominations, such as the Lutheran Church—Missouri Synod and the Christian Reformed church, the struggle for laywomen representatives on legislative bodies lasted into the 1960s and 1970s. Women in the Church of God (Cleveland, Tennessee) and the Church of Christ are still struggling.

Interest in women's ordination, strangely enough, revived in the midst of the "feminine mystique" of the 1950s. The United Methodist and United Presbyterian churches both ordained women fully in 1956, though there is still strong opposition among some conservative Presbyterians against women pastors and ruling elders. Methodists had given local preachers' licenses to women again in 1919 and ordained them local elders in 1924, but full equality came in 1956. In 1964 the southern Presbyterians followed their northern compatriots. In 1970 the Lutheran Church in America and the American Lutheran Church both ordained women. The Free Methodist Church finally ordained women in 1974. The Episcopal church recognized women deacons on a par with men in 1970 but did not grant women the priesthood until 1976. The first woman became a rabbi in 1972. A few Southern Baptist women have been ordained. However, acceptance by local parishes has been slow, even though as many as 50 percent of the student bodies of some seminaries are women. Holiness denominations still have a much higher percentage of women clergy.

THE HOLINESS-PENTECOSTAL MOVEMENT

Fundamentalism infected those groups with Calvinist backgrounds most deeply; it made only modest inroads into Wesleyan denominations. The Holiness churches and the Pentecostal churches which they spawned grew rapidly through the ministry of a large cadre of women preachers. For example, in the 1890s one conference of the Nazarene church in western Tennessee consisted entirely of women preachers. Thirty percent of the Pilgrim Holiness Church's ministers were women in the early days of this century. The Pillar of Fire was founded by Alma White, wife of a Methodist Episcopal minister. She claimed to be America's first woman bishop. An ardent feminist, her periodical was entitled *Woman's Chains.* Amy Semple McPherson organized the Foursquare Gospel Church in 1927. In 1934 Evangeline Booth, daughter of Catherine and William, became international general of the Salvation Army.

Holiness and Pentecostal groups, however, became preoccupied with institution building—churches, denominational structures, publishing houses, colleges, even seminaries. In the beginning they despised seminary-educated ministers; now they coveted one for their own congregation. Begun often as churches of the urban poor, they were also becoming respectable, middle class. Women were again squeezed out of leadership by the values of the dominant culture. They were evangelists and missionaries, home and foreign, but they were not pastors of larger churches, denominational executives, or seminary professors.

A SOCIAL CONSCIENCE

Rebirth of an evangelical social conscience can be dated from the publication of Carl Henry's *Uneasy Conscience of Modern Fundamentalism* (1947) and Sherwood Wirt's *Social Conscience of the Evangelical* (1968). The latent movement was nourished by magazines such as *The Other Side,* initially concerned with racism, and the *Post-American* (now *So-*

journers), devoted to issues of racism, militarism, poverty, and community.

Then, in 1973, Evangelicals for Social Action was convened in Chicago. Primarily concerned with racism, greed, and militarism, the by-invitation-only group of seventy-five Christian leaders included three women: Sharon Gallagher, then editor of *Right On* (now *Radix*); Eunice Shatz, founder of Chicago's Urban Life Center to give evangelical college students exposure to the inner city, and Nancy Hardesty, writer and graduate student. With prompting, the group included the statement which prefaces this chapter in the Chicago Declaration, their statement of social principles. When asked why he declined to sign the statement, evangelist Billy Graham specifically cited this paragraph as the one with which he most directly disagreed.

Hardesty was selected to serve on the executive committee to plan the group's 1974 Thanksgiving Conference. Women and blacks were to be specifically included this time, but on a quota basis. The nucleus of women invited, all committed to feminism as well as other social issues, formed the Evangelical Women's Caucus. A group from the Washington, D.C., area agreed to host a national convention, which was held Thanksgiving weekend, 1975. At the same time in Chicago, Hardesty and Lucille Sider Dayton, with a support group centered at North Park Seminary (Evangelical Covenant Church), founded a biblical feminist newsletter entitled *Daughters of Sarah*. EWC has now grown into a national organization which has held five national coventions in sites ranging from Saratoga, New York, to Seattle, Washington. The movement represents a revival of the biblical feminism which informed the first women's movement.

The movement has not yet come full circle. No longer present is the Finneyites' optimism and courage to take on the deep needs of our social order. Many women both inside and outside religious circles are concerned solely with their own gains. They want their own rights, not human rights for all persons. They are concerned only about their own standard of living and not the quality of life on this planet. Many women have read so many honest critiques of Christianity—from Elizabeth Cady

Stanton to Mary Daly—that they have lost sight of the God before and beyond religion.

Yet there is hope. Women are recovering a new spirituality. In the church they are modeling a new concept of ministry, speaking a richer theological language, offering new understandings of Scripture, raising important ethical issues of relationship as well as principle. In the world women and men together are finding new ways to implement peace, nurture our planet, make society a better home for the generations to come after us. The cord is unbroken; the river flows on.

APPENDIX: DEFENSES OF WOMAN'S MINISTRY

A Chronological Listing

An Oration Delivered on the Fourth Day of July 1800 by a Citizen of the United States to Which Is Added The Female Advocate Written by a Lady. Springfield, Mass.: Henry Brewer, 1808.

Crocker, Hannah Mather. *Observations on the Real Rights of Women with Their Appropriate Duties Agreeable to Scripture, Reason and Common Sense.* 1818.

Peirce, Deborah. *A Spiritual Vindication of Female Preaching, Prophesying, or Exhortation.* Carmel, N.Y.: Printed for Nathan Roberts, E. Burroughs, Printer, n.d.

Livermore, Harriet. *Scriptural Evidence in Favor of Female Testimony in Meetings for the Worship of God.* 1824.

Major, Sarah Righter. Pamphlet. 1835. Reprinted in Donald F. Durnbaugh. "She Kept on Preaching." *Messenger* (Church of the Brethren) 124 (April 1975): 18-21.

Grimké, Sarah M. *Letters on the Equality of the Sexes and the Condition of Woman.* Boston: 1838; reprint, New York: Burt Franklin, 1970.

Brown, Antoinette L. "Exegesis of 1 Corinthians, xiv, 34, 35; and 1 Timothy, ii, 11,12." *Oberlin Quarterly Review* 3 (July 1849): 358-73.

Foote, C. C. "Woman's Rights and Duties." *Oberlin Quarterly Review* 3 (October 1849): 383-408.

Mott, Lucretia. "Discourse on Woman." 17 December 1849. Reprinted in Anna Davis Hallowel. *James and Lucretia Mott: Life and Letters.* Boston: Houghton Mifflin Co. 1884, pp. 487-506.

Wilson, Elizabeth. *A Scriptural View of Woman's Rights and Duties, in All the Important Relations of Life.* Philadelphia: W. S. Young, Printer, 1849.

Price, Abby. "Women in the Church." *Proceedings of the Woman's Rights Convention, Held at Syracuse, September 8th, 9th & 10th 1852.* Syracuse: Printed by J. E. Masters, No. 26, Malcolm Block, 1852.

Lee, Luther. *Woman's Right to Preach the Gospel* (A Sermon Preached at the Ordination of the Rev. Miss Antoinette L. Brown, at South Butler, Wayne County, N.Y., September 15, 1853). Syracuse: Published by the Author, 1853. Reprinted in Luther Lee. *Five Sermons and a Tract.* Edited by Donald W. Dayton. Chicago: Holrad House, 1975.

Philanthropos. "Paul versus Silencing Woman." *Una* 1 (December 1853): 186-87.

Palmer, Phoebe. *Promise of the Father; or, A Neglected Speciality of the Last Days.* Boston: Henry V. Degen, 1859; reprint, Salem, Ohio: Schmul Publishing Co., n.d.

Booth, Catherine Mumford. *Female Ministry; or, Woman's Right to Preach the Gospel.* London: 1859; reprint in expurgated form, London: Morgan & Chase, n.d.; in *Papers on Practical Religion.* London: International Headquarters, 1890; New York: The Salvation Army Supplies Printing and Publishing Department, 1975.

Kellison, Barbara. *The Rights of Women in the Church.* Dayton: Printed at the Herald and Banner Office, 1862.

Brown, O. E. "Women Preachers." *New York Evangelist,* 24 July 1872, p. 234; 31 July 1872, p. 242.

Sherman, David. "Woman's Place in the Gospel." Preface to John O. Foster, *Life and Labors of Mrs. Maggie Newton Van Cott.* Cincinnati: Hitchcock and Walden, 1872.

Boardman, Mrs. W. E. (Mary). *Who Shall Prophesy?* Boston: Henry Hoyt, 1873.

Loomis, H. *May a Woman Speak in a Promiscuous Religious Assembly?* Pamphlet of an article from *Congregational Quarterly,* April 1874.

Brown, W. K. *Gunethics; or, The Ethical Status of Woman.* New York: Funk & Wagnalls, 1887. He also authored a book entitled *The Scriptural Status of Woman.*

Black, W. C. *Christian Womanhood.* Nashville: Publishing House of the Methodist Episcopal Church, South; J. D. Barbee, Agent, 1888.

Willard, Frances. *Woman in the Pulpit.* Boston: D. Lothrop Company, 1888. Reprint, in *Women and the Church in America.* American Theological Library Association, 1977. Microfiche.

Godbey, W. C. *Woman Preacher.* Louisville: Pentecostal Publishing Co., 1891.

Roberts, B. T. *Ordaining Women.* Rochester, N.Y.: Earnest Christian Publishing House, 1891.

Woolsey, Louisa M. *Shall Women Preach? or The Question Answered.* Caneyville, Ky.: 1891.

Rishell, Charles W. *The Official Recognition of Woman in the Church.* Cincinnati: Cranston & Stowe; New York: Hunt & Eaton, 1892.

Gage, Matilda Joslyn. *Woman, Church and State.* Chicago: Charles H. Kerr & Co., 1893.

Gordon, A. J. "The Ministry of Woman." *Missionary Review of the World* 7 (December 1874): 910-21; reprinted as a Gordon–Conwell Monograph, #61.

Sellew, W. A. *Why Not? Appeal for the Ordination of Those Women Whom God Has Called to Preach the Gospel.* North Chili, N.Y.: Earnest Christian Publishing House, 1894.

Franson, Fredrik. *Prophesying Daughters.* Minneapolis, Minn.: Johnston and Lundquist's book and Job Printers, 1896, in German; reprint, trans. Sigurd F. Westberg, *The Covenant Quarterly* 34 (November 1976): 21-40.

Rees, Seth C. *The Ideal Pentecostal Church.* Cincinnati: M. W. Knapp, 1897.

Willing, Jennie Fowler. "Woman in Gospel Evangelism." *Guide to Holiness* 64 (January 1896).

———. "God's Great Women." *Guide to Holiness* 67 (December 1897).

———. "Woman and the Pentecost." *Guide to Holiness* 68 (January 1898).

———. "Women Under the Pentecostal Baptism." *Guide to Holiness* 70 (February 1899).

Cooke, Sarah A. "Shall Women Preach the Gospel?" in *The Handmaiden of the Lord.* Chicago: S. B. Shaw, Publisher, 1900, pp. 174-76.

Bushnell, Katharine. *God's Word to Women.* Piedmont, Oakland, Calif.: Published by the Author, n.d.; reprint, Ray B. Munson, Box 52, North Collins, N.Y., 1976.

White, Alma. *Woman's Ministry.* Zarephath, N.J.: Pillar of Fire Publishers, n.d.

Booth, Evangeline. *Woman.* New York: Fleming H. Revell Co., 1930.

NOTES

Quotations cited throughout the text are taken from the original sources. Reprint sources are cited for the reader's convenience.

1. WOMAN OF THE CENTURY

Primary and secondary materials on Frances Willard are voluminous. She tells her own life story in *Glimpses of Fifty Years* (Chicago: Woman's Temperance Publication Association, 1889; reprint, New York: Hacker, 1970); in *Woman and Temperance* (Hartford, Conn.: Park Publishing Co., 1883; reprint, Salem, N.H.: Arno, 1972); and in *A Great Mother: Sketches of Madam Willard* (Chicago: Woman's Temperance Publishing Association, 1894). Another source much in Willard's own words is Anna A. Gordon's *The Beautiful Life of Frances E. Willard* (Chicago: Woman's Temperance Publishing Association, 1898). Willard's defense of woman's ministry is *Woman in the Pulpit* (Boston: D. Lothrop Co., 1888; reprint, Washington, D.C.: Zenger Publishing Co., 1976; microfiche, American Theological Library Association, *Women and the Church in America,* 1977).

The standard biography is Mary Earhart's dissertation, *Frances Willard* (Chicago: University of Chicago Press, 1944). Most recent is Ruth Bordin's *Woman and Temperance: The Quest for Power and Liberty, 1873–1900* (Philadelphia: Temple University Press, 1981). See also Lydia Trowbridge, *Frances Willard of Evanston* (Chicago: Willett, Clark & Co., 1938).

Willard wrote of her experience of holiness in S. Olin Garrison, ed., *Forty Witnesses* (1888: reprint, Freeport, Pa.: The Fountain Press, 1955) and in an obituary of her father, "Faith Victorious," which she contributed to the *Guide to Holiness* (June 1868).

Material concerning Hannah Whitall Smith is found in Willard's *Woman and Temperance;* Ray Strachey, *Frances Willard* (New York: Fleming H. Revell Co., 1913); Ray Strachey, *A Quaker Grandmother: Hannah Whitall Smith* (New York: Fleming H. Revell Co., 1914); and Robert Allerton Parker, *The Transatlantic Smiths* (New York: Random House, 1959).

Willard's speeches to the WCTU are published in the Union's *Minutes* of each annual meeting available on microfilm in the

Temperance and Prohibition Papers, published by the Michigan Historical Collections, The Ohio Historical Society, and the WCTU.

A final note concerning Willard's charismatic leadership: while biographers have been reluctant to term Willard a lesbian, it is clear, as Ruth Bordin puts it: "Women liked Willard. Indeed she was more than liked, she was loved, she was adored. Her intense, almost sexual attractiveness to members of her own sex was a major factor in her success." Mary Earhart is also rather candid in her chapter entitled "Friends and Companions." Anna Gordon herself, who destroyed many of Willard's letters and papers, quotes Frances's sister-in-law and former schoolmate Mary Bannister Willard's rather telling observation that Frances was not one to go for moonlight walks with the "university boys," as the other girls were wont to do. "A young man would have been temerity itself who would have suggested such a thing to her. In fact, she came to be something of a 'beau' herself—a certain dashing recklessness about her having as much fascination for the average schoolgirls as if she had been a senior in the University." Willard herself toward the end of *Glimpses* notes that "the loves of women for each other grow more numerous each day" and speaks of households where there are " 'two heads in counsel,' both of which are feminine," who have clasped hands and "taken each other 'for better or for worse.' "

2. THE WHOLE AGE MUST COOPERATE

For extended discussion of the changes in family life see Paul E. Johnson, *A Shopkeeper's Millennium: Society and Revivals in Rochester, New York, 1815–1837* (New York: Hill & Wang, 1978); Mary P. Ryan, *Cradle of the Middle Class: The Family in Oneida County, New York, 1790–1865* (Cambridge: Cambridge University Press, 1981); and Barbara Leslie Epstein, *The Politics of Domesticity: Women, Evangelism, and Temperance in Nineteenth-Century America* (Middletown, Conn.: Wesleyan University Press, 1981).

"Woman's sphere" is described by Nancy F. Cott, *The Bonds of Womanhood: "Woman's Sphere" in New England. 1780–1835* (New Haven: Yale University Press, 1977); Ann Douglas, *The Feminization of American Culture* (New York: Alfred A. Knopf, 1977; paper, New York: Avon, 1978); and Barbara Welter, *Dimity Convictions: The American Woman in the Nineteenth Century* (Athens: Ohio University Press, 1976). Welter's essay "The Cult of True Womanhood: 1820–1860" originally appeared in *American Quarterly* 18 (Summer 1966): 151-74, and has been reprinted in several anthologies.

Rebecca Harding Davis's *Life in the Iron Mills; or The Korl Woman* has been reprinted by The Feminist Press (Old Westbury, N.Y., 1972), with an introduction by Tillie Olsen, who includes that introduction and an excerpt from the book in *Silences* (New York: Delacorte Press, a Delta/Seymour Lawrence Edition, Dell Publishing Co., 1965, 1972, 1978).

Concerning the nineteenth century in general, most helpful are

Daniel Boorstin, *The Americans: The National Experience* (New York: Random House, 1965); Arthur M. Schlesinger, Jr., *The Age of Jackson* (Boston: Little, Brown & Co., 1945); and Alice Felt Tyler, *Freedom's Ferment* (New York: Harper & Row, Publishers, Harper Torchbooks, 1944; reprint, Salem, N.H.: Arno, n.d.).

3. A CURE FOR "BETWEENITY"

This book is based on my doctoral dissertation, " 'Your Daughters Shall Prophesy': Revivalism and Feminism in the Age of Finney" (University of Chicago, 1976). Many of the specific quotations used from this chapter on are documented there.

The primary source for the life of Charles Finney is his *Memoirs* (New York: A. S. Barnes & Co., 1870; reprint, New York: AMS Press, 1977). Best modern edition with introduction is his *Lectures on Revivals of Religion*, edited by William G. McLoughlin (Cambridge, Mass.: The Belknap Press of Harvard University Press, 1960). McLoughlin is the author of several works on revivalism, *Modern Revivalism* (New York: The Ronald Press Co., 1959) and *Revivals, Awakenings, and Reform* (Chicago: The University of Chicago Press, 1978). Whitney E. Cross also published a helpful analysis of the Second Great Awakening in *The Burned-Over District: The Social and Intellectual History of Enthusiastic Religion in Western New York, 1800–1850* (New York: Harper & Row, Publishers, Harper Torchbooks, 1950; reprint, New York: Octagon, 1981). For a more recent analysis of Presbygational theology, see George H. Marsden, *The Evangelical Mind and the New School Presbyterian Experience* (New Haven: Yale University Press, 1970).

Other recent works on Finney include dissertations by James E. Johnson, "The Life of Charles Grandison Finney" (Syracuse University, 1959), and Garth Rosell, "Charles Grandison Finney and the Rise of the Benevolence Empire" (University of Minnesota, 1971). Donald W. Dayton in *Discovering an Evangelical Heritage* (New York: Harper & Row, Publishers, 1976) brings together the Oberlin milieu of Christianity, holiness, and reform.

A convenient source of information on all American women who died before 1950 is *Notable American Women, 1607–1950*, Edward T. James, Janet Wilson James, and Paul S. Boyer, editors. 3 vols. (Cambridge, Mass.: The Belknap Press of Harvard University Press, 1971).

Robert Samuel Fletcher wrote *A History of Oberlin College*. 2 vols. (Oberlin: Oberlin College, 1943; reprint, Salem, N.H.: Arno, 1971).

Concerning Weld and the Grimkés one can read *Letters of Theodore Dwight Weld, Angelina Grimké Weld and Sarah Grimké, 1822–44*, edited by Gilbert H. Barnes and Dwight L. Dumond. 2 vols. (New York: Appleton-Century-Crofts, 1934; reprint, Gloucester, Mass.: Peter Smith, 1965; New York: Da Capo Press, 1970); Sarah Grimké, *Letters on the Equality of the Sexes and the Condition of Woman* (1838;

reprint, New York: Burt Franklin, 1970); Angelina Grimké, *Letters to Catherine [sic] E. Beecher, in Reply to An Essay on Slavery and Abolitionism* (Boston: Isaac Knapp, 1838; reprint, Salem, N.H.: Arno, 1969). Biographies of the trio include Gilbert H. Barnes, *The Anti-Slavery Impulse, 1830–1844* (New York: Harcourt, Brace & World, A Harbinger Book, 1933, 1964; reprint, Gloucester, Mass.: Peter Smith, n.d.); Robert H. Abzug, *Passionate Liberator: Theodore Dwight Weld and the Dilemma of Reform* (New York: Oxford University Press, 1980); Gerda Lerner, *The Grimké Sisters from South Carolina* (New York: Houghton Mifflin Co., 1967; paper, New York: Schocken Books, 1971); and Katharine DuPré Lumpkin, *The Emancipation of Angelina Grimké* (Chapel Hill: The University of North Carolina Press, 1974).

A source which makes connections similar to those made in this chapter is Alice S. Rossi's *The Feminist Papers* (New York: Columbia University Press, 1973; Bantam Books, 1974), especially in "Part 2—Pioneers on a Moral Crusade: Feminism and Status Politics."

4. "BE YE HOLY!"

No modern biography of Phoebe Palmer has been written, the only one being Richard Wheatley's *The Life and Letters of Mrs. Phoebe Palmer* (New York: W. C. Palmer, Jr., Publisher, 1876). The standard histories of the holiness movement are by Melvin Easterday Dieter, *The Holiness Revival of the Nineteenth Century* (Metuchen, N.J.: Scarecrow Press, 1980); Charles Edwin Jones, *Perfectionist Persuasion: The Holiness Movement and American Methodism, 1867–1936* (Metuchen, N.J.: Scarecrow Press, 1974); Timothy L. Smith, *Revivalism and Social Reform* (Nashville: Abingdon Press, 1957; New York: Harper & Row, Publishers, 1965; reprint, Gloucester, Mass.: Peter Smith, n.d.; Baltimore: Johns Hopkins, 1980); Vinson Synan, *The Holiness-Pentecostal Movement in the United States* (Grand Rapids: Wm. B. Eerdmans Publishing Co., 1971).

Barbara Zikmund's dissertation at Duke University (1969), "Asa Mahan and Oberlin Perfectionism," is helpful, as are Donald W. Dayton's "Asa Mahan and the Development of American Holiness Theology," *Wesleyan Theological Society Journal* 9 (Spring 1974): 60-69 and Edward A. Madden and James E. Hamilton's *Freedom and Grace: The Life of Asa Mahan* (Metuchen, N.J.: The Scarecrow Press, 1982).

5. RELIGION IS SOMETHING TO DO

Elizabeth Cady Stanton tells her own story in *Eighty Years and More: Reminiscences 1815–1897* (1898; reprint, New York: Schocken Books, 1971). Other sources include Theodore Stanton and Harriot

Stanton Blatch, *Elizabeth Cady Stanton: As Revealed in Her Letters, Diary and Reminiscences.* 2 vols. (New York: Harper & Brothers, 1922; reprint, Salem, N.H.: Arno, 1977); Lois W. Banner, *Elizabeth Cady Stanton: A Radical for Women's Rights* (Boston: Little, Brown & Co., 1980); Alma Lutz, *Created Equal: A Biography of Elizabeth Cady Stanton, 1815–1902* (New York: The John Day Co., 1940; reprint, New York: Octagon, 1973); and Henry B. Stanton, *Random Recollections* (New York: Harper & Brothers, 1887).

Elizabeth Cazden has written a new biography of *Antoinette Brown Blackwell* (Old Westbury, N.Y.: The Feminist Press, 1983), drawing on Mrs. Claude Gilson's manuscript "Antoinette Brown Blackwell: The First Woman Minister," along with Brown letters and manuscripts at the Schlesinger Library, Radcliffe College, and papers in the Library of Congress. Elinor Rice Hays also wrote *Those Extraordinary Blackwells* (New York: Harcourt, Brace & World, 1967).

Catherine Booth's story is told in *The Life of Mrs. Booth: The Mother of the Salvation Army* by F. de L. Booth-Tucker. 2 vols. (London: The Salvation Army Printing Works, 1892).

6. DIRECTLY TO THE BIBLE

Sources on the life of Lucy Stone include Alice Stone Blackwell, *Lucy Stone: Pioneer of Woman's Rights* (N.p.: Published by Alice Stone Blackwell Committee, 1930; reprint, Detroit: Gale Research Co., 1971; Millwood, N.Y.: Kraus Reprints, n.d.); Elinor Rice Hays, *Morning Star: A Biography of Lucy Stone, 1818–1893* (New York: Harcourt, Brace & World, 1961), as well as Hays's *Those Extraordinary Blackwells.*

Primary source for the woman's rights movement is *The History of Woman Suffrage.* 6 vols. (vol. 1, New York: Fowler & Wells, Publisher, 1881; and vol. 2, Rochester: Susan B. Anthony, 1881; reprint, Salem, N.H.: Arno, 1969), edited primarily by Stanton and Anthony and thus describing their viewpoint. See also the sources listed in chapter 11.

7. THE UNCTION MAKES THE PREACHER

The Appendix contains a partial list of nineteenth-century defenses of woman's ministry.

8. AIM AT BEING USEFUL

The *Autobiography of Lydia Sexton* was published in Dayton, Ohio, by the United Brethren Publishing House, 1882.

One of the earliest and best books on women in American church history was R. Pierce Beaver's *All Loves Excelling* (Grand Rapids:

Wm. B. Eerdmans Publishing Co., 1968, revised and reissued in 1980
as *American Protestant Women in World Mission: A History of the First
Feminist Movement in North America.)*

The Benevolence Empire is described in such books as Ray Allen
Billington, *The Protestant Crusade, 1800–1860* (New York: Macmil-
lan, 1938; reprint, New York: Times Books, 1976); John R. Bodo, *The
Protestant Clergy and Public Issues, 1812–1848* (Princeton: Princeton
University Press, 1954; reprint, Philadelphia: Porcupine Press, n.d.);
Charles C. Cole, Jr., *The Social Ideas of the Northern Evangelists
1826–1860* (New York: Octagon Books, 1966); Charles I. Foster, *An
Errand of Mercy: The Evangelical United Front 1790–1837* (Chapel
Hill: The University of North Carolina Press, 1960); Clifford Griffin,
*Their Brothers' Keepers: Moral Stewardship in the United States,
1800–1865* (New Brunswick, N.J.: Rutgers University Press, 1960);
Joseph R. Gusfield, *Symbolic Crusade: Status Politics and the
American Temperance Movement* (Urbana: University of Illinois
Press, 1963, paper, 1972; reprint, Westport, Conn.: Greenwood Press,
1980). More contemporary, and feminist, interpretations of reform
are cited in the following chapters.

9. THE BONDS OF SISTERHOOD

In addition to Barnes's *The Antislavery Impulse, 1830–1844,* see
Aileen S. Kraditor, *Means and Ends of American Abolitionism:
Garrison and His Critics on Strategy and Tactics, 1834–1850* (New
York: Random House, Vintage Books, 1967, 1969); Keith E. Melder,
*Beginnings of Sisterhood: The American Woman's Rights Movement
1800–1850* (New York: Schocken Books, 1977); and Blanche
Glassman Hersh, *The Slavery of Sex: Feminist-Abolitionists in
America* (Urbana: University of Illinois Press, 1978).

10. FEMALES WHO HAVE DEVIATED FROM
THE PATHS OF VIRTUE

Most helpful are Barbara J. Berg, *The Remembered Gate: Origins of
American Feminism, the Woman and the City, 1800–1860* (Oxford:
Oxford University Press, 1978) and Carroll Smith Rosenberg, *Religion
and the Rise of the American City: The New York City Mission
Movement, 1812–1870* (Ithaca, N.Y.: Cornell University Press, 1971).

11. TO TOUCH IT WAS CONTAMINATION

Sources on Willard are cited in chapter 1. Recent studies of
temperance and woman's rights include Ruth Bordin, *Woman and
Temperance: The Quest for Power and Liberty, 1873–1900,* and
Barbara Leslie Epstein, *The Politics of Domesticity: Women,
Evangelism, and Temperance in Nineteenth-Century America.*

On suffrage, in addition to *History of Woman Suffrage,* the standard sources are Eleanor Flexner, *Century of Struggle: The Woman's Rights Movement in the United States* (Cambridge, Mass.: The Belknap Press of Harvard University Press, 1975); Aileen S. Kraditor, *The Ideas of the Woman Suffrage Movement, 1890–1920* (Garden City, N.Y.: Doubleday & Co., Anchor Books, 1965; reprint, New York: W. W. Norton & Co., 1981); and Miriam Gurko, *The Ladies of Seneca Falls: The Birth of the Woman's Rights Movement* (New York: Schocken Books, 1976).

12. MUTUAL SUBMISSION, ACTIVE DISCIPLESHIP

Ernest Sandeen traces the demise of evangelicalism in *The Roots of Fundamentalism: British and American Millenarianism, 1800–1930* (Chicago: The University of Chicago Press, 1970; paper, Grand Rapids: Baker Book House, 1978). The essence of his argument is also found in *The Origins of Fundamentalism: Toward a Historical Interpretation* (Philadelphia: Fortress Press, Facet Books, 1968), which reprints an essay originally published as "Toward a Historical Interpretation of the Origins of Fundamentalism" in *Church History* 36 (1967): 66-83. See also George Marsden, *Fundamentalism and American Culture: The Shaping of Twentieth-Century Evangelicalism, 1870–1925* (New York: Oxford University Press, 1980).

The history of Methodist women is traced in Hilah F. Thomas, Rosemary Skinner Keller, and Louise L. Queen, editors, *Women in New Worlds: Historical Perspectives on the Wesleyan Tradition.* 2 vols. (Nashville: Abingdon Press, 1981, 1982).

Sources in the new evangelical or biblical feminism include Letha Scanzoni and Nancy Hardesty, *All We're Meant to Be: A Biblical Approach to Women's Liberation* (Waco, Tex.: Word, 1974; rev. ed., Nashville: Abingdon Press, 1985); Donald W. Dayton, *Discovering an Evangelical Heritage;* Virginia Ramey Mollenkott, *Women, Men, and the Bible* (Nashville: Abingdon Press, 1977), *Speech, Silence, Action! The Cycle of Faith* (Nashville: Abingdon Press, 1980); *The Divine Feminine: The Biblical Imagery of God as Female* (New York: Crossroad, 1983); Paul Jewett, *Man as Male and Female* (Grand Rapids: Wm. B. Eerdmans Publishing Co., 1975) and *The Ordination of Women* (Grand Rapids: Wm. B. Eerdmans Publishing Co., 1980); Virginia Hearn, editor, *Our Struggle to Serve: The Stories of Fifteen Evangelical Women* (Waco, Tex.: Word, 1979); and Patricia Gundry, *Woman Be Free* (Grand Rapids: The Zondervan Corp., 1977), *Heirs Together* (Grand Rapids: The Zondervan Corp., 1980), and *The Complete Woman* (New York: Doubleday & Co., 1981).

INDEX